STAINED GLASS BASICS

TECHNIQUES
TOOLS
PROJECTS

✦

CHRIS RICH

WITH MARTHA MITCHELL AND RACHEL WARD

Sterling Publishing Co., Inc. New York
A STERLING/LARK BOOK

Art Direction: Dana Irwin
Production: Dana Irwin, Celia Naranjo, and Kay Stafford
Illustrations: Orrin Lundgren
Photographer: Evan Bracken

Library of Congress Cataloging-in-Publication Data
Rich, Chris, 1949-
    Stained glass basics : techniques / tools / projects / by Chris Rich,
  with Martha Mitchell and Rachel Ward.
        p.   cm.
    "A Sterling/Lark Book."
    Includes index.
    ISBN 0-8069-4876-0
    1. Glass craft.   2. Glass painting and staining.   I. Mitchell, Martha.
  II. Ward, Rachel.   III. Title
  TT298.R53   1996
    748.5--dc20   95-54102
                                                            CIP

10 9 8 7 6 5 4 3 2 1

A Sterling/Lark Book

Published by Sterling Publishing Company, Inc.
  387 Park Ave. South, New York, NY 10016

Created and produced by Altamont Press, Inc.
  50 College Street, Asheville, NC 28801

© 1996, Altamont Press

Distributed in Canada by Sterling Publishing, c/o Canadian Manda Group,
  One Atlantic Avenue, Suite 105,
  Toronto, Ontario, Canada M6K 3E7

Distributed in Great Britain and Europe by Cassell PLC, Wellington House,
  125 Strand, London, England WC2R OBB

Distributed in Australia by Capricorn Link (Australia) Pty Ltd.,
  P.O. Box 6651, Baulkham Hills Business Centre, NSW 2153, Australia

Printed in Hong Kong

ISBN 0-8069-4876-0

COVER: THE STAINED GLASS PANEL DEPICTED ON THE COVER
WAS DESIGNED AND MADE BY STEVE MCLESTER OF ASHEVILLE, NORTH CAROLINA.

TABLE of CONTENTS

Chris

When, after a lapse of 20 years, I decided to take up stained glass crafts again, I set out enthusiastically to buy a how-to book that would refresh my skills. To my distress, I couldn't find one. For

weeks I waded through pattern books and tomes for studio artists, but what I wanted—a book that included step-by-step practice sessions on cutting glass and assembling projects, advice on buying tools and materials, and a collection of well-designed patterns—didn't seem to be available. I did find something even better, however: two of the most skilled, generous, and devoted glass artisans I've ever known—Marty Mitchell and her daughter, Rachel Ward.

The three of us decided to create the book I couldn't find. Marty and Rachel are glass artisans and teachers; I'm a writer. I had the questions; they had the answers—and their answers made sense. *Stained Glass Basics* is the result.

A good teacher, we believe, does more than tell her students what to do. She demonstrates every critical step. A good how-to book works the same effect. Because we couldn't package Marty and Rachel within these pages, we've filled the pages with photos of their hands at work.

Good teachers also leave their students with skills that can be used outside the classroom. By the time you've made a few of the projects in this book, you'll be well equipped to begin working with almost any stained glass pattern available on the market. Trust us: If you love glass and are eager to learn, you'll be creating stained glass panels, boxes, lamps, and suncatchers in no time.

Marty

A love of drawing and painting; the simple mirth of light passing through bottles of colored water; the creation of playful tissue-and-glue collages for childhood windows; the inspiration of leaded glass transoms in aging Victorian homes; and the fairyland magic of beveled glass entryways gleaming warmly on snowy nights. These things—and the perfect sparrow panel I purchased for my mother—made the offer of a stained glass class irresistible. Working with glass has been a joy, passion, love, and career ever since.

While my seventeen years as a professional glass artist have refined my skills, my basic responses to the medium are much the same as they were when I started.

—Soul-singing ecstasy as light passes through colored glass, and as colors, values, textures, and densities combine to form a living palette

—Essential recognition in the elegant purity of a defining lead line

—And, always, a sense of gratification in the tangible product created with these materials.

I hope that this book will be the catalyst that brings you to a similar experience.

Rachel

My introduction to stained glass came early. Intrigued by the sparkling colored images of my mother's work, I designed and executed my first simple project when I was eleven. It hangs in our studio to this day. In the eighth grade, I made a glass map of Magellan's voyage, and during my junior year in high school, I made my first commissioned piece. What a blessing to discover that I could make a living doing something I loved!

Because the majority of our work is commissioned, our range of subjects and sizes is very wide indeed. I still find, however, that my sense of accomplishment and satisfaction is just as great when I make a small suncatcher as it is when I construct an elaborate window. The fantastic palette of colors and textures with which we "paint" our designs is a source of joy in and of itself. To then experience the interplay of glass and ever-changing cycles of light is nothing short of magical!

RACHEL AND MARTY

All Three of Us

Stained Glass Basics is designed to provide you, the novice, with a step-by-step guide to making beautiful stained glass projects. With its help, you'll build a solid foundation of skills and knowledge, one upon which you'll continue to build as long as you enjoy this wonderful craft.

Stained glass can provide endless technical challenges for hobbyists and professionals alike, but we don't want to mire you down in technical talk here! We would like to tell you that this medium is capable of inspiring a range of emotions, from the awe experienced in front of a grand cathedral window to the simple cheer created by a tiny suncatcher.

Working with glass can even sharpen your perceptions of the world around you. Take note of the delicate shading of a flower, hold in your mind an image of an especially breathtaking sunset, take in the landscapes and images of your daily life. Let these observations and emotions breathe life into your stained glass work. View the world through rose-colored glass—and blue, and green, and violet, and ...

tained-glass work isn't complicated, but before you plunge into making your first project, take a good look at this section. In it, we've sketched an outline of the steps required to make both copper foil and leaded glass panels. Think of this overview as a mental file cabinet, filled with folders in which you can store what you learn from the rest of this book.

Copper Foil Panels

First you'll cut pieces of glass to match a pattern, and then you'll wrap their edges with thin strips of metallic foil (see Photo 1).

To help keep the corners of the panel at right angles as you assemble it, you'll build a jig on top of the pattern. Then you'll arrange the foiled glass on the pattern, apply flux to the seams, and melt some solder onto the seams to hold the pieces of glass together (see Photo 2).

Next, you'll melt solder to cover each seam completely, on both sides of the panel (see Photo 3). These solder beads will form the linear design of your panel and will provide its structural framework.

To create a border, you'll cold-solder the panel's four edges, as shown in Photo 4. (Borders may be framed in zinc or lead came instead; you'll learn how to do this in Chapter 8.)

Finally, you'll make hooks, attach them to your piece, clean the finished panel, and display it (see Photo 5).

The copper foil method results in a finely "drawn" line quality and lends itself to smaller, more intricately shaped pieces. Its finished appearance, filled with details, is organic in nature. To maintain the flow of this line quality, it helps to remember that each step effects the subsequent steps. A finished solder seam will reflect how carefully you prepared your paper pattern and cut your glass, how accurately you applied the copper foil, and, of course, how smoothly you soldered it.

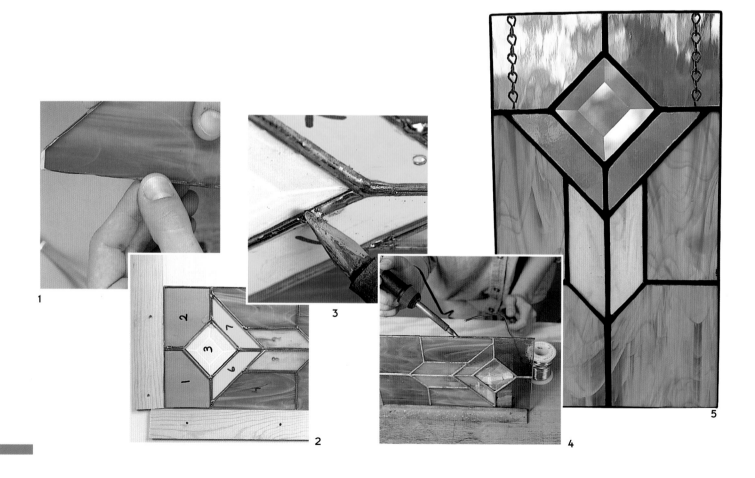

1

2

3

4

5

Leaded Glass Panels

To make a leaded glass panel, you'll begin by cutting the pieces of glass, making an assembly jig on top of your pattern, and positioning two pieces of border came against the jig strips (see Photo 6).

Then you'll shape and cut pieces of lead came to fit around each piece of glass as you assemble the panel (see Photo 7).

After adding the last two pieces of border came and checking the panel dimensions, you'll flux and solder every joint on both sides of the panel in order to bind the lengths of came and the border together (see Photo 8). You'll also make hooks and solder them in place.

To strengthen the panel, you'll brush glazing compound under the flanges of the lead (see Photo 9).

To remove the flux from the soldered joints and to clean the excess glazing compound from the panel, you'll brush the panel with patching plaster or a similar powder and scrape away excess compound from the edges of the lead flanges (see Photo 10).

Then you'll give the panel a final cleaning before applying a finishing compound and displaying your completed project (see Photo 11).

Leading, unlike copper foil fabrication, creates a bold drafted line quality that is perfectly suited to geometric and larger, softly curvilinear designs. While you may find that the leading process is more tolerant of minor cutting discrepancies, a good bit of precision is still required.

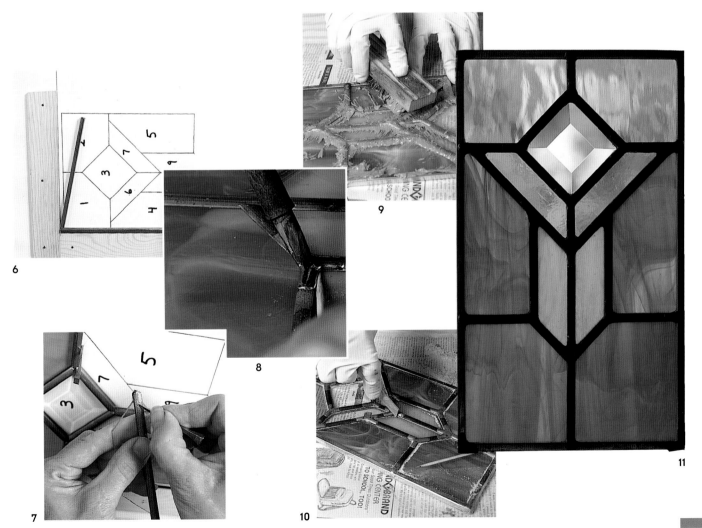

6

7

8

9

10

11

Chapter One: Art Glass

You don't need an encyclopedic understanding of glass to start making well-crafted stained glass projects, so don't study this chapter as if it were textbook material. Browse through it at your leisure and refer to it whenever you need a bit of specific information.

A real knowledge of glass—its appearance, texture, ease of cutting, and cost—comes with experience. The more you indulge your fascination with this wonderful material and the more projects you make, the quicker that knowledge will come. In the meantime, tell the people who work in your local stained glass store that you're a beginner. If you bring your project pattern along with you, these folks will be glad to lend you a hand selecting glass.

You'll be amazed by the many types and colors of art glass available. Hold a few sheets up to different kinds of light and compare and contrast the effects. Enjoy the feel of each sheet; run your fingers across its surface and familiarize yourself with its texture. Line a few sheets up in a window to get a sense of how colors affect one another.

If your community doesn't boast a stained glass retail shop or friendly studio, contact a few retail glass suppliers; you can get their names and addresses by asking for help at the reference desk of your local library. Request copies of these suppliers' retail catalogues, which are often packed with useful information.

How Glass is Made

Art glass is made by combining sand, silica, soda ash, recycled glass, and lime at extremely high temperatures. Added metal oxides provide color; cobalt and chromium, for example, yield blue. The molten mixture is formed into flat sheets by using one the following methods:

Mouth-blown antiques are created by gathering the molten glass at the ends of a long pipe and then blowing the glass into a cylinder. This cylinder is flattened into a sheet by removing its ends and cutting it along its length. The sheet is then annealed (cooled slowly) to remove its brittleness.

Drawn (also called **new** or **sheet**) **antique glass** is similar to mouth-blown glass but is made by machine. The molten glass is drawn vertically through a refractory block to form it into sheets.

Rolled glass, as its name implies, is made by rolling molten glass into sheets. There are three methods for doing this: rolling the molten glass by hand on a large table; ladling the glass onto a flat surface and rolling the sheets by machine; or using a machine to roll a continuously flowing stream of molten glass. Color combinations are created by swirling molten glass of one color into another before the glass is annealed.

Types of Glass

Glass professionals often divide all art glass into two main categories: **cathedrals** and **opalescents** (or opals). Cathedrals—of which there are many types—are usually transparent and are valued for their ability to transmit light. They vary in thickness, depending on how heavily textured they are, and in ease of cutting.

Opals, which can be either machine-rolled or hand cast, are characterized by their milky, semitranslucent look, created by including materials that cause the glass to crystallize. Solid color opals are available, but mixed opals, made by swirling one or more colors of molten glass together before rolling the sheets, are more common.

Usually more difficult to cut than cathedrals, opals are excellent glasses to use in lamp shades because they tend to reflect more light than they transmit and therefore disguise the harsh glare of lit bulbs. Color patterns and degrees of light transmission vary from sheet to sheet, although contemporary glass manufacturers make great efforts to see that color formulas remain consistent.

Within these two general categories are dozens of types of glass, some made only by particular manufacturers. Following are descriptions of some of the more common varieties. Once you can distinguish these from one another by sight, you'll know you're an expert, but remember, you don't need to be one to enjoy stained glass crafts!

Keep in mind as you read these descriptions that although the terms we've used here are fairly common, stained glass terminology may vary from manufacturer to manufacturer and from studio to studio.

Types of Glass

Full antique glass is not necessarily old glass, but the technique used to make it is very similar to that used centuries ago. A mouth-blown glass which varies in thickness and therefore in color intensity within each sheet, it has attractive surface striations and often includes air bubbles as well.

Semi-antique glass, unlike full antique, is clear and uniform in color, and because it isn't mouth-blown, tends to be more consistent in thickness.

Bevels are pieces of clear or softly colored glass with flat surfaces and angled borders. The beveled edges of these lovely pieces refract light to create elegant rainbow effects. Bevels come in a wide variety of geometric shapes, but **clusters** (groupings of bevels) are also available.

Crackle is a translucent full antique glass distinguished by a scale-like pattern that may remind you of alligator skin. This texture is made by dipping the hot blown cylinder of glass in water to create fissures.

Drapery glass, which is hand rolled, is aptly named for the deep folds on its surface. You'll know this glass when you see it; the sheets resemble draped garments.

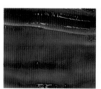

Flashed glass is a full antique made by dipping a thicker base layer of glass, which is often clear or light in color, into another color of hand-blown glass, usually brighter in color. By sandblasting or etching the flashed (thinner, brighter) layer, striking two-tone effects can be achieved. Always score flashed glass on the thicker base layer.

Glue chip, a popular translucent glass, has a distinctive pattern reminiscent of winter frost on a window. The pattern is created by sandblasting cathedral glass and applying hot animal-hide glue to it. As the glue dries, it peels away flakes of glass to create the distinctive glue-chip look.

Iridescent glass is cathedral or opalescent glass which has been coated with a thin layer of metallic salts. As its name suggests, iridescent glass shimmers with color, much as a rainbow does.

Jewels are pieces of glass which have been cast to resemble cut gems. They come in a variety of sizes and colors and are most attractively used as highlights.

Nuggets (also called **globs**) are unevenly shaped pieces of glass with flat bottoms and rounded upper surfaces. They're often used as accents.

Reamy glass is an antique glass with dramatic, fluid textures and sweeping curves. Almost celestial in appearance, "reamies" also include impressive air bubbles, which vary widely in shape and size. When cutting reamies, always avoid cutting through these bubbles.

Ring mottled glass, an opalescent, derives its name from the small circular patterns on its surface. The patterns are of greater opacity than the surrounding glass.

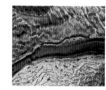

Ripple glass is characterized by its boldly undulating surface texture.

Rondels (also **roundels**) are mouth-blown disks of antique glass made by twirling a molten glass bubble on the end of a blow pipe to flatten it. Distinguished by the knobs in their centers, rondels are usually translucent and come in many sizes and colors. The machine-made versions are known as pressed rondels.

Seedy glass, a cathedral, comes in many colors, and is distinguished by the seedlike air bubbles in it.

Streaky glass is a multicolored glass made by mixing, but not blending, two or more cathedral glasses.

The Cost of Glass

Those of you who are artists will know that some painting pigments are more expensive than others. The same is true for some of the substances used to create color in glass. Some ruby-colored glasses, for example, are made by adding gold; you'll see this fact reflected in their price!

Even professional glass cutters are sometimes a little intimidated by expensive glass, so don't feel alone if you notice that your hands are shaking the first time you approach a truly costly sheet. Breathe deeply. Then score and break off a small end piece and use it to make several experimental cuts to get a feel for the characteristics of the glass. Remind yourself, too, that glass breaks! It's the nature of the beast. We'd venture to guess that every glass artist in the world has broken a piece of glass now and then.

As a beginner, you may be tempted to avoid buying the more expensive types of glass. We don't mean to destroy your budget, but if that budget can handle one bit of excess, let it be a piece of costly glass—the piece that captures your heart the minute you see it—to serve as a highlight for your first project.

Selecting Glass

We have two good reasons for not telling you which types and colors of glass to buy for the projects in this book. First, we don't want to deprive you of the fun; selecting glass can be tremen-

dously exciting. Second, no glass studio stocks every type of glass, so we'd just be setting you up for frustration if we told you which types to buy. We'll offer you a few tips, though, to make your glass selecting easier.

■ To find color combinations that are pleasing, line up a few scraps of glass against a sunny window so you can see how the different colors effect one another.

■ Evaluate the lighting conditions in which your panel will be displayed. A panel filled with dark cathedral glass, for example, will look much better with strong back-lighting than it will in a dark room.

■ Small projects can be swamped by the use of too many colors. Select one or two dominant colors and use various shades or textures of those colors instead. Try choosing one multicolored sheet and then selecting other sheets to echo the colors in it.

■ Bold colors can be startlingly dramatic—or just plain "too much." To soften their effect, place them next to lighter colors or next to clear textured glass.

■ When selecting glass for lamp shades, choose opals for most sections and cathedrals for use as highlights. The opals will block the harsh light of the burning bulb and will disguise unsightly hardware, while the cathedrals will sparkle like jewels.

■ Think about the relative positions and sizes of different color areas in your pattern design.

■ Consider the function of your finished panel. Cathedrals may suit a door overlooking your garden, but you probably wouldn't want to use many of them in a panel designed for a bathroom window.

Chapter Two: Workshop and Safety

Although professional stained glass artists often work in large studios, you won't need a huge workshop to create the projects in this book. What you will need is a space that meets the basic requirements described in this chapter. You'll also want to familiarize yourself with the safety guidelines we've included. Working with lead, solder, and patinas needn't endanger your health, but they will if you handle them carelessly.

One special message to pregnant women: Spend the next few months planning your projects and cutting glass, but wait until after delivery and nursing to work with lead or solder!

Work Space Requirements

■ The space that serves as your studio, humble and small though it may be, must have good overhead lighting. Poor lighting invites poor work habits as well as accidents. We wish we could tell you that accidents don't happen, but they do. If you can't stand the sight of blood, you may want to think twice about this hobby!

■ Don't ever work in an area in which food is prepared, stored, or served. Ingesting lead is dangerous. The farther your work space is from your kitchen, the better.

■ Make sure your space has at least one electrical outlet with a grounded circuit. You'll use it to plug in your soldering iron and, if you choose to purchase one, your glass grinder.

■ Glass must be cut on a steady, level surface. Either construct a sturdy, waist-high workbench with a flat plywood surface (see Figure 1) or cover a sturdy table or a counter with a plywood work board. (For more information on work boards, turn to page 29.) This board is easy to replace when it becomes too pitted or

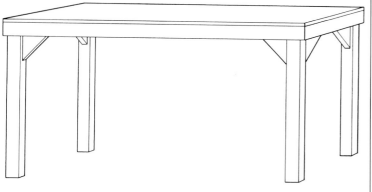

Figure 1

rough, and will also serve as a convenient way to transport or reposition your projects.

■ Sheets of glass placed on uneven surfaces are likely to crack, so keep your bench or board clean. Use a soft-bristled bench brush— regularly—to sweep away glass shards and slivers.

■ Glass slivers and chips will eventually find their way to the floor, so be sure its surface is hard and easy to mop.

■ Store sheets of glass vertically to help prevent breakage. Placing sheets of paper between them will also protect them from scratching each other. Building a glass-storage bin isn't difficult (see Figure 2), but old wooden crates also work well. Sheets of glass may even be propped up at a slight angle against a wall, with a flat sheet of cardboard or wood underneath them to keep them from chipping.

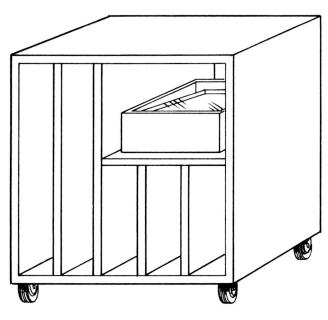

Figure 2

■ Keep all glass-storage bins below shoulder level so you never have to lift glass above your head. Organize your sheets of glass by color and also by size; you're likely to cut yourself as you try to grasp a small piece of glass that is sandwiched between larger ones. Don't arrange the sheets too tightly together.

■ When possible, store lengths of lead came without bending them. Ask your local supplier for an empty came shipping carton and place this long cardboard box right on the floor. If space is at a premium, construct a wooden bin that is half the length of the came you purchase (see Figure 3) and cut the came in half before

placing it inside. A dowel hanger (see Figure 4) will also work; just drape the lengths of came over it, being careful not to twist them when you do. To prevent the lead from oxidizing, cover or wrap the came with newspaper.

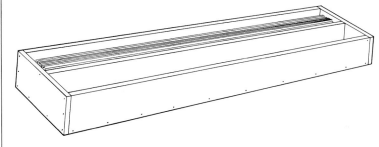

Figure 3

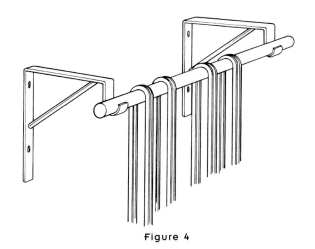

Figure 4

■ Good ventilation in your workshop is a must. Both soldering and patina application produce toxic fumes, so be sure to work in a well-ventilated area with a fan to draw away fumes.

■ You'll need some sort of access to running water. Many hobbyists simply transport their small projects back and forth to the nearest tub or sink, but if you choose to do this, clean the basins thoroughly before immersing your body or any food in them.

■ Except for brushing glass slivers off the surface of your work bench or board, never sweep, dust, or use a household vacuum cleaner in your work space. These activities will spread lead dust into every corner—something to be avoided at all costs! Clean floors with damp mops and other surfaces with damp rags.

■ Keep track of your tools by putting them back where they belong rather than scattering them on your work surface. The simple tool rack shown in Figure 5 on the next page is easy to make and will hold a number of hand tools within easy reach.

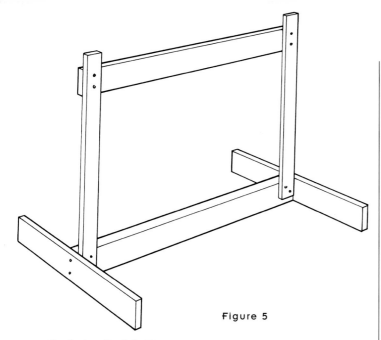

Figure 5

Safety Guidelines

■ The dangers of ingesting or inhaling lead or permitting it to enter your bloodstream can be serious. Never, under any circumstances, allow youngsters or animals to enter your work or lead-storage areas unless you have nothing to do but make sure that they don't touch any lead, solder, flux, patina, or glass.

■ Assemble a comfortable set of clothes and a closed, comfortable pair of shoes. Wear these when you work with stained glass—and at no other time.

■ Wash your hands thoroughly every time you stop work. Use a good cream or pumice hand-cleaner first to remove as much lead as possible from your skin. Then follow up by washing with soap and water, scrubbing your fingernails thoroughly as you do. When you're through for the day, take a shower, wash your hair, and scrub those hands again.

■ Never eat, drink, or smoke cigarettes while working with or around lead. Keep your hands away from your mouth and face until you've washed up.

■ Cover all open cuts, scratches, and scrapes with bandages. Healthy skin won't absorb lead, but broken skin will.

■ Wear a tight-fitting dust mask when working with lead. You must avoid inhaling airborne particles.

■ Don't use your palms to wipe off your bench or board. One careless swipe with your hand may leave your palm filled with glass splinters. (If you break an expensive piece of glass, bang your head on the wall if you must, but don't wring your splinter-covered hands!)

■ Always wear safety glasses when cutting glass, using a grinder, or working with flux and solder. If you should get a splinter of glass in your eye, don't rub! Glass slivers will usually rest flat on your iris and can be rinsed away by running clean water over your open eye. If thorough rinsing doesn't work, see a doctor right away.

■ To pick up a large sheet of glass, grasp it with both hands at its top edge and keep it perpendicular to the floor as you lift it. This way, if the glass slips or cracks, it won't slice your palms. If you do drop a sheet of glass, never grab for it. Let go, and jump back quickly.

■ Keep the floor of your work space clean and free of clutter. Prevent accidents by making sure there's nothing to trip you up as you move from one area to another.

■ Wear rubber gloves whenever you handle patinas.

■ Stay alert. Working with glass when you're tired or irritable is not the route to success—or to safety!

■ When accidents with glass happen (and let's face it, they do) you'll be glad to have a well-stocked first-aid kit on hand. Check the kit periodically to see that it's filled with bandages (including butterfly bandages for deep cuts), sterile gauze, disinfectants, and tape. If you burn yourself on a soldering iron or hot solder, apply ice right away. Then, as an alternative to traditional creams, try coating the burn with the viscous liquid from a slit aloe leaf; aloe prevents blistering. You may find that essential oil of lavender takes the "ouch" out, too.

Chapter Three: Materials and Supplies

here may come a day when you'll want to stock all the materials and supplies described in this chapter, but until that time, you'll save a good bit of money by purchasing only what you need for what you want to make. On page 72, you'll find lists of what you'll need to make copper foil panels, what you'll need to make leaded glass panels, and what you'll need to make both.

Lead Came

The metal framework for leaded glass panels consists of a network of lead came that is soldered at every joint. This structure serves several purposes: It holds the glass together, provides a semirigid support for the panel, and is the linear portion of the panel's design.

Lead came, usually sold in 4' or 6' (122 or 184 cm) lengths, comes in a variety of sizes and contours, but the two basic profiles are U-shaped came (used to form borders for both copper foil and leaded glass projects) and flat or rounded H-shaped came (most often used in the interior portions of leaded designs).

In leaded glass projects, each glass piece abuts the heart of the came surrounding it (see Figures 1 and 2). Note that in most instances, this heart is approximately 1/16" (1.5 mm) thick, no matter how wide the came. For this reason, the pattern lines in leaded glass patterns are usually assumed to be 1/16" wide.

Until you've practiced cutting and shaping lead came, buy about 25 percent more than you think you need.

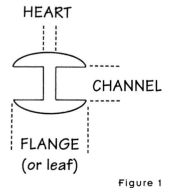

HEART

CHANNEL

FLANGE
(or leaf)

Figure 1

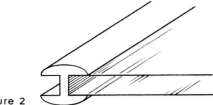

Figure 2

Zinc or Brass Came and Brass Channel

Zinc and brass cames are also available. U-shaped zinc came, which is rigid, makes an excellent border for straight-sided projects; unlike lead, it won't stretch or sag over time. Brass channel, also less malleable than lead, is frequently used in three-dimensional projects such as lamps and boxes.

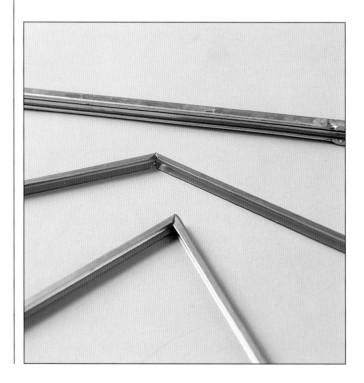

Copper Foil

In copper foil projects, each piece of glass is wrapped with a thin, flexible, adhesive-backed strip of copper, which serves as a base for the solder that binds the project together.

Copper foil comes in a variety of widths and is usually sold in 36-yard (32.9 m) rolls. The most common widths are 3/16", 7/32", and 1/4" (4.6, 5.4, and 6 mm). Which width to use? Beginners will find that 7/32" foil is attractive, easy to apply, and wide enough to cover the edges of most types of glass, even those with very irregular surfaces.

Once you reach the stage at which you're designing your own patterns or adapting existing patterns, your choice of foil will depend on both practical and aesthetic considerations. The foil must be wide enough to cover the cut edge of the glass you're using and to extend around to its front and back surfaces; very narrow foil may not work on thick glass with irregular surfaces. If the design of your pattern cries out for delicate seams, use a narrow foil. For dramatic, heavy-lined

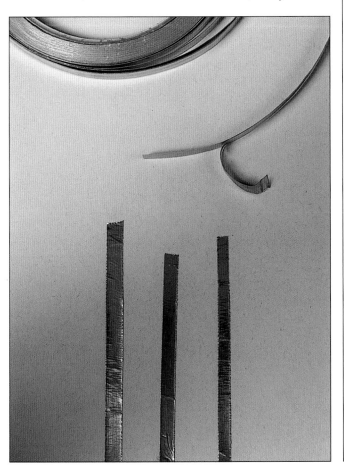

designs, select wider foils. By all means combine foil widths in a project, too, by wrapping some pieces in wide foil and others in narrow.

Copper foil is also used to create overlays. These are design lines or shapes created by applying foil, wire, or sheet metals right on top of the glass rather than around its edges. For instructions on working with overlays, see pages 73-74.

The most popular foils are copper colored on their adhesive-backed inner surfaces, but if you'd rather not see this copper color in the finished project, you can purchase special foils with black or silver inner surfaces.

Copper Restrip and Copper Wire

Copper restrip, available from stained glass shops and suppliers, comes in coils and looks a bit like copper foil, but unlike foil is relatively stiff. Cut to length and inserted between foiled pieces of glass before the seams of the project are soldered, restrip serves to strengthen potential weak spots in foil constructions.

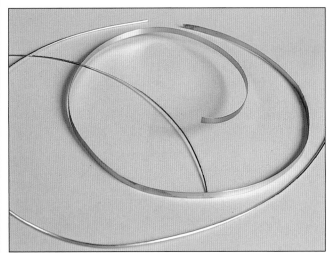

For making hooks (see pages 57, 64, and 65), reinforcing copper foil projects (see page 83), and creating special effects (see page 86), nothing can beat copper wire, which is available either uncoated or pretinned. To tin (or coat with solder) plain copper wire, just apply flux and a thin layer of solder.

Solder

Stained glass soldering is the art of joining the foiled pieces of glass or the pieces of lead in a project. In leaded projects, the solder serves to hold the pieces of came together at their junctures; in copper foil projects, the solder covers the foiled seams completely.

The type of solder necessary for stained glass work has a solid (not an acid) core and is an alloy of tin and lead. If you buy solder at a hardware store rather than from a stained glass supplier, read the label carefully. When melted with a soldering iron, this solder, which usually comes in 1-pound (453.6 g) spools, will adhere to copper foil or to lead, brass, or zinc came.

Two primary types of stained glass solder are available: 60/40 solder, which is 60 percent tin and 40 percent lead; and 50/50 solder, which is made up of equal proportions of tin and lead. Each type has its advantages. 60/40 solder has an especially shiny finish and a lower melting point. Because it solidifies quickly, it's excellent for decorative soldering and overlay work. 50/50 solder, on the other hand, with its higher melting point, is less likely to remelt and leak through the cracks between foiled pieces when the opposite side of the project is soldered. In addition, when you're soldering copper foil seams, 50/50 won't freeze so quickly that the soldered seams have ridges in them. Because 50/50 stays liquid longer, you won't have to work quite as quickly as you would with 60/40.

Lead-free solders are available; you may want to experiment with these if you're hesitant to work with lead.

Flux and Flux Brush

Flux is applied to the lead or foil just before soldering; it helps disperse the heat from the iron, cleans the metal, and allows

TECH TIP

FLUXING MIRRORS

The cut edges of mirrored glass must be sealed before applying flux or patina, or these substances will leak under the silvered surface and damage it. After cutting the mirror, clean it under running water; do not use glass cleaner. Dry well, and apply two coats of clear lacquer to the mirror back and edges, allowing ample drying time after each coat.

the solder to flow smoothly and "stick" to the lead or foil. Without flux, you'll find it impossible to create smooth attractive solder joints. Instead, the solder will form ugly porous peaks.

Flux is available in both paste and liquid form. Paste flux is somewhat sticky and, as you dab it onto copper foil projects, tends to lift and shift the glass pieces. You'll do better to use liquid flux on copper foil constructions, but if you want to use paste flux instead, dab it on each foiled piece as you lay out the pieces on the pattern. Paste flux is generally easier to use on leaded glass projects.

To apply liquid flux, first decant a little into a small container so that you're less likely to spill it. (Decanting is unnecessary with paste flux.) Dip the flux brush into the container and stroke the brush along the copper foil seams. Paste flux is applied in a similar fashion.

The flux must be removed as soon as you've finished soldering, as it tends to haze (or cloud) glass and, if left on lead or foil, will eventually cause oxidation. Commercial flux removers are available but aren't absolutely necessary. Liquid dishwashing detergent and water will remove liquid flux from copper foil projects; paste fluxes can be removed from both copper foil and leaded projects by brushing them with patching plaster (see the next page).

Glazing Compound

Exterior leaded glass projects, such as panels for windows and doors, must be glazed (or puttied) on both sides in order to insulate them, make them waterproof, and strengthen them.

Indoor projects should also be glazed to strengthen them, prevent rattling, and provide a finished appearance.

Glazing compounds made specifically for leaded glass are available, but the ordinary gray glazing compound used to glaze metal windows is perfectly acceptable when thinned to the consistency of thick brownie batter. Transfer the compound to an empty coffee can, mix in a few drops of mineral spirits or paint thinner, and stir well with a paddle (if you're strong!) or an electric drill and paint-stirring bit. To darken the compound—an optional step—mix in a bit of lamp black. The thinned compound should barely hold a peak. If it's too thick, you won't be able to work it under the flanges of the came. If it's too thin, it will ooze out from under the flanges before it has had a chance to dry.

Powdered Patching Plaster, Plaster of Paris, or Whiting

Fluxes and glazing compounds leave residues on glass. To remove these, to seal the glazing compound under the flanges of the came, and to clean up the came on leaded glass projects, you'll sprinkle your glazed project with patching plaster, whiting (calcium carbonate), or plaster of paris, and brush the powder vigorously over the glass.

Scrub Brushes

Keep several thick-bristled scrub brushes, large or small, in stock. You'll use them to brush glazing compound under the flanges of the came, to brush patching plaster over soldered panels in order to remove any flux left on their surfaces, and to scrub your panels clean with water and dishwashing detergent. Cycle the brushes through these different processes until

they're so caked with glazing compound or so worn that they're unusable. To keep the glazing brushes pliable, store them with their bristles submerged in mineral spirits or paint thinner.

Lattice Strips and 3/4" (1.9 cm) Brads

To hold square and rectangular panels in alignment as you assemble them, you'll build a jig by nailing two lengths of lattice at right angles to one another, right onto your work board or bench surface. Purchase several feet of 1/4" x 1-1/2" (.6 x 3.8 cm) lattice and a small box of brads at your local lumberyard or home center.

Horseshoe Nails

As you assemble pieces of glass in leaded glass projects, you'll hold them in place by pounding horseshoe nails into your work board or bench surface. One dozen nails should be sufficient for even the largest of panels; the nails can be reused many times.

Craft Paper, Carbon Paper, and Tracing Paper

For making patterns and templates, get a few large sheets of heavy-weight craft paper, a brown paper similar to, but stiffer than grocery-bag paper. For designing your own patterns and for tracing existing ones, purchase tracing paper from an art-

or craft-supply store or from a blueprint shop. (For creating designs on tracing paper, use artist's charcoal, which is easily erased with a dry rag.)

A few large sheets of carbon paper will come in handy for tracing patterns, although copying large or complex patterns at a blueprint or photocopy shop may be easier.

Glue Stick and Spray Adhesive

To affix craft-paper templates securely to your glass, use a water-soluble, white glue stick. (Rubber cement will work, too, but the templates won't adhere as well during grinding.)

Instead of tracing your patterns onto craft paper, you can also use spray adhesive to glue a photocopy or blueprint of the pattern onto the craft paper and then cut your templates by cutting through both sheets at once.

Duct Tape or Masking Tape

Masking or duct tape will keep patterns in place on work boards and will hold together the components of three-dimensional projects, such as lamps, as you solder them.

Fine-Tipped Waterproof Marker and Light-Colored Paint Pen

When working with complex patterns and multiple templates, it's all too easy to mix up your pieces of glass. For this reason, you'll use a marker to write a number and code on every template. When you remove the templates from the cut glass pieces, you'll mark the glass itself with either a waterproof marker or, on dark glass, a light-colored paint pen.

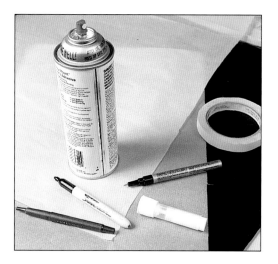

Patina, Neutralizer, and Rubber or Latex Gloves

Patinas are chemical solutions of water, copper sulfates, and mineral acids. When they're applied to solder, most patinas change its color to either copper or black.

Patinas are acids; wear gloves when you work with them! Purchase disposable surgical gloves at a medical supply store or pharmacy, or buy a pair of rubber gloves at your local hardware store. To prevent the patina bottle from tipping over on your bench or work board, wrap a piece of lead came around its bottom. Also avoid inhaling patina fumes.

Patinas should not be allowed to sit on glass. Wash your project right after application, using a commercial neutralizer or a mixture of dishwashing detergent, baking soda (sodium bicarbonate), and water.

Patina application is entirely optional. If you find that you don't like its look once you've applied it, just remove it by rubbing the solder with fine-grade steel wool.

Steel Wool

Oxidation leaves an unsightly white substance on solder. The best way to remove this (and an essential step before applying patina to foiled seams or joints) is to rub the affected area with fine-grade steel wool. Steel wool will also pick up the oozing foil adhesive after copper foil panels are soldered.

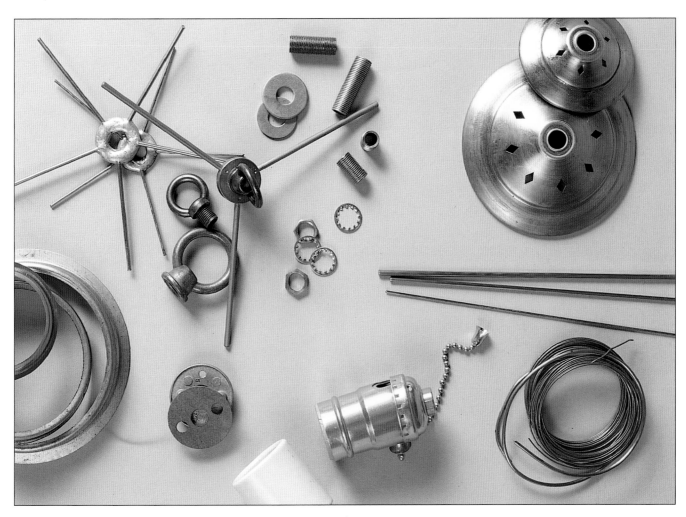

Rags

Soft, lint-free, cotton rags (diapers work well) will come in handy for wiping glass clean, applying patinas, lubricating glass cutters, and polishing projects after they've been brushed with whiting.

Lamp Supplies

Stained glass lamp shades require fittings, many of them available through glass, lamp, or electrical suppliers.

■ Vase caps are the circular brass caps affixed to the open tops of the shades. These caps help to hold the glass panels together and permit the lamp to be suspended or placed on a lamp base. Be sure to purchase caps with ventilation holes in them, as trapped heat from burning bulbs may damage the glass and soldered seams.

■ Spiders are brass rings with arms extending from them; they sometimes replace caps. Spiders may also be used in conjunction with caps to provide additional support. Although spiders are available commercially, they're easy to make by soldering lengths of brazing rod to brass washers.

■ Lamp hardware, cords, and electrical switches are a must for fully assembled lamps. Purchase ceramic sockets; the metal versions have paper liners that tend to disintegrate from the higher temperatures under glass shades.

■ Lamp bases are widely available through specialty lamp companies and stained glass suppliers.

■ Brass brazing rod and washers are used to make custom spiders.

Hinge Materials and Fine-Link Chain

Hinges for glass boxes may be made from hollow tubing and brazing rods; you'll find the former at craft shops and the lat-

ter at electrical-supply or hardware stores. Fine-link chain, which is carried by many home centers, is usually added to boxes in order to prevent the lids from pulling away the copper foil as they bend backwards.

Chain, Screw Eyes, and S-Hooks

Many glass panels look their best when suspended in front of a window on two lengths of sturdy chain. Slip an S-hook through each end of each chain. Then slip the upper S-hooks into screw eyes installed at the top of the window and the lower S-hooks into handmade hooks affixed to the panel.

Glass Cleaner

Any commercial glass cleaner that does not contain ammonia will work well on stained glass.

Newspaper

Several layers of newspaper will provide a cushion between your work surface and the sheet of glass you intend to cut. (A low-pile carpet remnant also works well.) It's especially important to protect glass that is uneven in texture, as the hard surface of your bench or work board, combined with the pressure you exert as you score the glass, might otherwise cause the glass to crack. When you're finished cutting, just roll up the paper, along with the glass splinters and chips on it, and discard.

You'll also cover your work board or bench with newspapers when you're glazing leaded panels. If you don't, hardened bits of glazing compound will solidify on the work surface, making it too uneven to support glass sheets safely. Take the same precaution when applying patinas.

Finishing Compound

Commercial finishing compounds provide a protective, transparent coating over your finished project. They help prevent oxidation of the lead and/or solder and make dusting an easy job. A high-quality car wax is a good substitute.

Chapter Four: Tools and Equipment

Beginners in any craft often make the mistake of thinking that high-tech tools will guarantee success. The truth is that owning a huge collection of implements just isn't necessary. Let restraint be your motto. Start by buying only the tools accompanied by a ✦ in the following pages. After you've learned to use these tools and are confident that you'd like to pursue stained glass crafts, add other tools as you need them.

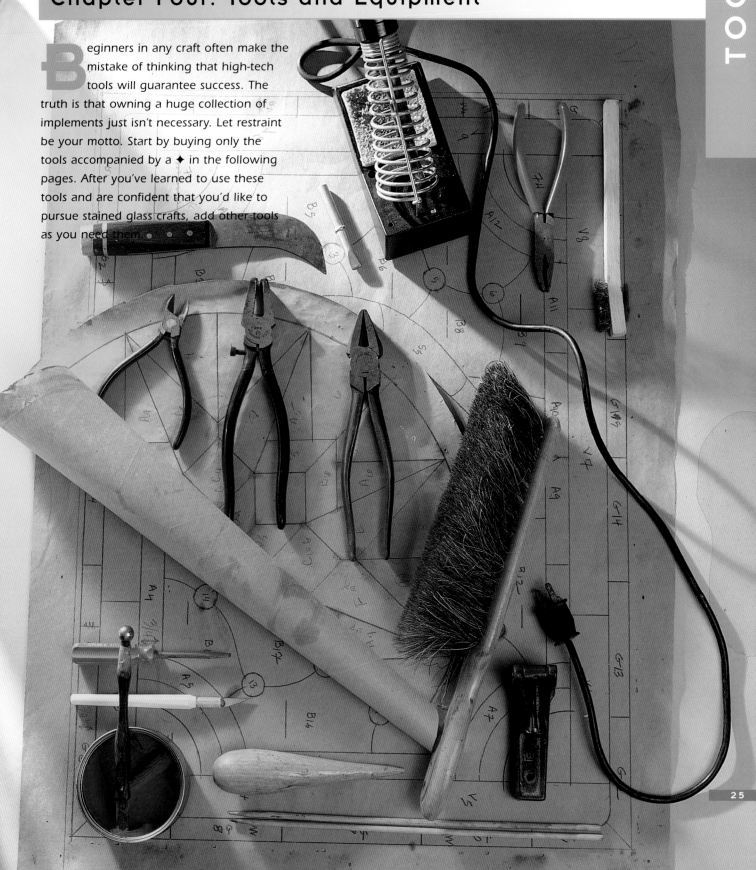

Some of the projects in this book require the use of one or more tools that won't be in your basic set. To simplify matters, we've listed these along with the projects in Chapter 10. Don't forget to check these lists before you tackle a project; there's nothing more frustrating than discovering halfway through construction that you're missing something critical.

✦ Soldering Iron, Stand, Sponge or Rag, and Sponge Holder

The soldering iron used in stained glass work is not the typical gun-shaped iron used for soldering electrical components. A stained glass iron is stick-shaped and consists of a heat-resistant handle fitted with a replaceable tip about the length and thickness of a finger. Purchase your iron from a glass studio or supplier and get a 1/4" (6 mm) or 3/8" (1 cm) tip to go with it.

Some irons come with rheostats that allow you to adjust their temperatures. The temperatures of other irons are controlled by the specific tips inserted into their handles. For the projects in this book, either type of iron will work well.

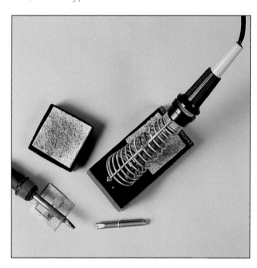

Do buy or make a stand for your iron. Commercial stands range from heavy-duty coiled versions to small pieces of shaped metal. The coiled stands not only prevent the hot iron from touching your work surface but also protect your hands and nearby objects. Less costly stands protect the work surface only. The least expensive stands are homemade; a coat hanger bent to shape will work, as will an X-shaped stand made by hammering two nails at angles into your work surface.

Some stands include a well for a damp, natural-fiber sponge or damp cotton rag. Separate sponge trays are also available. You'll clean the hot tip of your iron by wiping it on this sponge or rag as you work.

✦ Glass Cutter, Rag, Tin or Jar, and Kerosene or Sewing-Machine Oil

Glass cutters come in all shapes and sizes, but their cutting action depends on the same simple mechanism: a small metal wheel, which is rolled across the glass in order to create a nearly invisible fissure called a **score**. The score weakens the glass so that it can be broken.

Most cutters are stick-shaped, but pistol-grip cutters, especially useful for people with limited hand strength, are widely available. Some cutters are self-lubricating; an internal well in the handle releases oil onto the wheel. Others must be lubricated by wiping the wheel across a rag soaked in kerosene or sewing-machine oil. Keep this moist rag in a container on your work surface.

Until you've acquired some glass-cutting experience, we recommend using one of the traditional, stick-shaped cutters sold at hardware stores. While these may not look fancy, don't have replaceable wheels, and don't last as long as more expensive cutters, they're very effective and won't put dents in your wallet when you need to replace them. (If you purchase another type of cutter, test a few models for comfort of grip.

See pages 34 and 35 for information on holding glass cutters.)

The three slots in the handle of a traditional glass cutter were originally used for grozing—nibbling away unwanted bits of

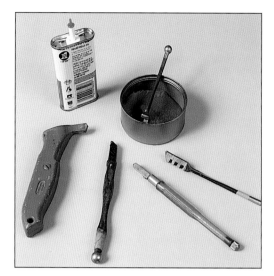

glass after cutting. Today, grozing pliers and glass grinders are more commonly used for this purpose.

Lead Vise

Unless lead came is stretched before it's used, it will sag from the weight of the glass in an assembled panel. There are several ways to stretch came without a vise. If you have a willing friend, each of you can grasp one end of the came with pliers and pull in opposite directions until the lead straightens. If you're temporarily friendless, you can hold one end of the came by stepping on it firmly, and pull the other end with a pair of pliers. Of course, you'll have to cut the came to a manageable length first. Closing a door over one end of the came while you pull on the other also works, but the lead will leave a noticeable dent in the door!

A lead vise will make your life easier. Attach the vise to your bench or to any stable surface. To use the vise, slip one end of the came into its jaws, with a channel facing up. Strike the hinged jaw with a hammer to ensure that its serrations dig down into the soft came. Next, untwist the came so that the same channel faces up along its length. Then grip the other end of the came with slip-joint pliers. (As the lead is being stretched, it may break or slip out of the vise, so position your body to one side of the pliers, not directly behind them.) Brace yourself by placing one leg behind the other, and pull

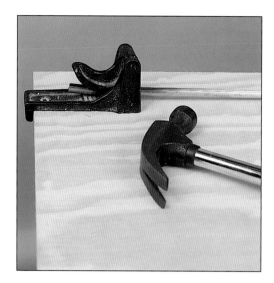

on the came until it is straight and taut. Try not to bend the came once you've stretched it.

✦ Lead Loppers or Lead Knife

Lead loppers (also known as lead cutters) have sharp narrow jaws, flat on one surface and concave on the other; these slice cleanly through lead came. Always turn the flat portion of the jaws toward the piece of lead you wish to save; the lead on the other side will be cut into a V shape as the jaws come together.

Loppers can cut lead came at sharp angles and are also used to separate the leaf from the heart of the came, sometimes necessary when you need to fill gaps or make repairs.

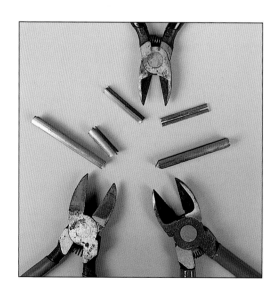

Some artists prefer lead knives to loppers. To use a lead knife on H-shaped came, place the came with one leaf up (or, in the case of U came, with the channel up) and rock the blade gently back and forth across the lead. Lead knives prevent waste because their blades don't cut came into a V shape on one side, as the jaws of loppers do.

✦ Lathekin

This tool serves two useful functions. You'll use it to open the leaves of stretched lead came so they're wide enough to accept the edges of cut glass pieces. It will also serve as a lever for lifting pieces of glass into lead channels as you assemble a project.

✦ Burnishers and Wooden Scrapers

Any number of "found" or handmade objects can be transformed into burnishers—the tools you'll use to burnish copper foil to glass. Small hardwood dowels work well, and bamboo skewers are perfect for burnishing foil over tight interior

curves. A wooden clothespin with one "leg" cut off not only makes a good burnisher, but may also be used for tapping pieces of glass into lead came.

Scraping excess glazing compound from the edges of lead leaves is best done with an implement that won't scratch the glass. Try a popsicle stick that's been cut at an angle at one end.

✦ Wire Brushes

Lead came oxidizes very quickly. Because solder won't adhere to oxidized lead, you'll use a wire brush from your stained glass supplier to clean all lead joints before soldering. (Don't use steel wool for this job; it will leave debris that may mix with the molten solder.)

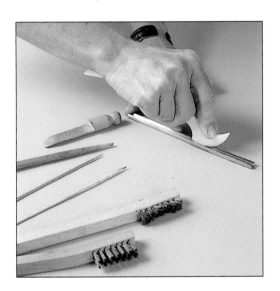

✦ Pattern Shears

These scissorlike implements, which come in two sizes, are used for cutting out **templates** (paper pattern pieces that represent each piece of glass in a project). Each size has blades designed to slice away a thin strip of paper as they cut—1/16" (1.5 mm) wide for leaded glass projects and 1/32" (.75 mm) wide for copper foil projects. This strip, which is discarded, represents the distance between the pieces of glass that will be occupied by the copper foil or the heart of the lead came—plus a little extra space to permit accurate positioning of the pieces during assembly.

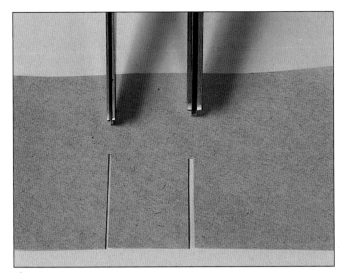

Breaking Pliers

These pliers, which come in both narrow- and wide-jawed versions, are used to break glass along the score made by a glass cutter. Their smooth, flat jaws grip the glass firmly without scratching it. For instructions on the use of these pliers, see Chapter 5.

Grozing Pliers

When their narrow jaws are manipulated correctly, grozing pliers will nibble away tiny fragments from the edges of glass pieces that have been cut too large. You may need to lubricate new grozing pliers, or you'll find them difficult to use. For instructions on the use of these pliers, see Chapter 5.

Combination Pliers

These pliers combine the functions of breaking and grozing pliers in a single tool. One jaw is usually flat and the other concave; both jaws are serrated.

Running Pliers

Designed to exert the same amount of pressure on each side of the score made by your glass cutter, running pliers are extremely efficient at breaking out long scores, whether straight or curved. Made of metal or plastic, these pliers have one concave and one convex jaw. By positioning the concave jaw directly over the score line and the convex jaw underneath it and then gently squeezing the jaws together, it's possible to exert the considerable force necessary to carry a break

over a long distance. Some running pliers have a mark on the upper jaw to guide you as you position the jaws over the score. Turn to page 38 to see how these pliers work.

Needlenose Pliers

While they're not essential, needlenose pliers will come in handy when bending copper wire into hooks, bending brazing rod to make box hinges, and shaping copper wire for wire overlays.

Slip-Joint Pliers

You'll use these ordinary household pliers for stretching lead came and for holding hooks as you solder them in place.

Work Board

Think of a work board as a small, portable bench. Placed on a sturdy table or counter, it will serve as a surface for cutting glass and assembling your panel. A 2' X 2' (61 x 61 cm) sheet of 5/8" (1.6 cm) or thicker plywood will do for small projects, but be sure that your work board is at least 2" (5.1 cm) larger than the project you're assembling.

Safety Glasses

Always wear these when cutting glass, using a grinder, or soldering.

Hammer

You'll need a small hammer for driving in the horseshoe nails that hold individual pieces of glass in place as a panel is being assembled and for constructing assembly jigs for straight-sided

CUTTING TOOLS

Figure 1 depicts an easy-to-make cutting square for scoring straight lines. Rest the inner horizontal edge of the tool against one straight edge of the glass sheet and use the vertical bar as a cutting guide. Just slide the tool along the sheet of glass to cut a series of strips.

Figure 2 shows a special jig for cutting strips of equal width. On a smooth hardwood or laminate board, nail three lath strips at right angles to one another. Slip the sheet of glass you wish to cut into place and place the fourth lath across the jig as shown. Next, position this fourth lath so it will guide the wheel of your glass cutter to score a strip exactly as wide as you need. (Remember, because the cutter head, not the wheel itself, will be touching the edge of this lath, the line you score will be a slight distance away from the lath edge.) Nail the fourth lath into place.

As you score the glass, press down on the lath above the sheet to prevent it from bowing away from the cutter. Slide the sheet out of the jig, break off the scored strip, and groze away any sharp lips on the sheet so it will sit squarely in the jig when you score the next strip. Reinsert the sheet to cut another strip of the same width. To change the width of the glass strips, just pry up the fourth lath, reposition it, and nail it down again.

panels. Lead hammers with plastic or rubber heads are available. These will not only drive nails, but can be used to tap glass pieces into place during leading.

◆ Scissors

Keep a sharp pair of scissors on hand for cutting along the outer perimeters of patterns and for cutting copper foil to length.

◆ Craft Knife

For trimming copper foil after you've wrapped it around a cut piece of glass, nothing works better than a craft knife fitted with a #11 blade. Keep extra blades handy and replace them frequently.

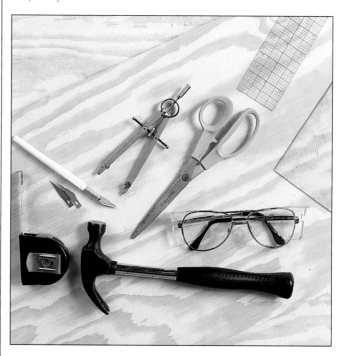

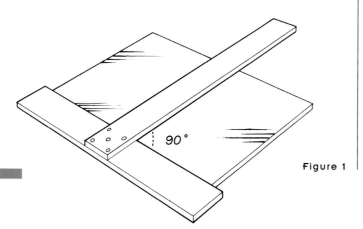

Figure 1

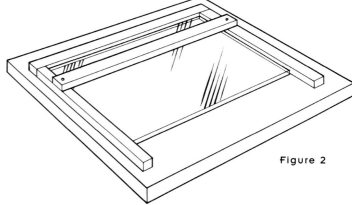

Figure 2

✦ Straightedge, Compass, Tape Measure, and Right Angle

These four tools are helpful for designing and measuring patterns, checking the dimensions of finished panels, and constructing assembly and cutting jigs.

✦ Glass Grinder

Although you can certainly make projects without owning a glass grinder, if stained glass is a hobby you're going to stick with, you're going to want to own one. This piece of equipment will grind away a multitude of cutting discrepancies. Its diamond-coated bit leaves a perfectly smooth and perpendicular edge on any piece of glass, an especially important bene-

fit when you're working with copper foil. Smooth, perpendicular glass edges will make it possible to foil your glass evenly and will thereby ensure evenly soldered seams on your finished panels.

To use the grinder, hold the glass firmly and press it against the water-lubricated bit, moving the glass back and forth to grind it to shape.

Most grinders also come with a smaller bit designed for grinding holes through glass and for grinding tight inside curves. To lubricate this smaller bit, which may not be moistened automatically, try positioning an intravenous drip to release water onto the bit as you work. We use this technique, and it's amazingly effective!

The one disadvantage to grinders is that they aren't inexpensive. If you can't afford one, don't despair. Stained glass artists have survived for centuries without this piece of equipment; patience and skillful grozing can take its place.

Light Box

A light box (see Figure 3) consists of a rectangular frame with a sheet of sandblasted, 1/4"-thick (6 mm) plate glass on top and a light within the frame. Some artists cut their glass by placing the cartoon on the plate glass, covering it with the glass to be cut, and guiding their glass cutter along the edges of the backlit pattern lines.

While this cutting method is fairly common, we firmly believe that only by cutting with templates (see Chapter 6) can you guarantee success. Templates leave no room for doubt or error. Cutting freehand over a light box requires exceptional skill and rarely results in cutting as accurate.

Light boxes have other uses, however, so you may wish to build one. They offer a reasonably good way of viewing glass with light behind it, and when you're cutting glass for complex patterns, viewing the pieces of glass on a light box will help you control the flow of color and texture from one piece to another. They're also very helpful for drafting and tracing patterns.

◆ Hacksaw

Zinc came (see page 18) is too stiff to be cut with lead loppers. Special electrical cutters are available, but a little elbow grease and a 32-tooth per inch (2.5 cm) hacksaw, will do the job just as well.

Motorized "Mini-Tool"

If you plan on doing a lot of stained glass work, purchase a handheld, motorized "mini-tool." This versatile piece of equipment comes with a wide variety of bits—from cutting blades that will slice right through zinc and brass, to wire brushes for removing oxidation from lead came.

Bench Vise

A bench vise is very useful for holding zinc came in position as you cut it to size. For information on alternative ways to brace the came, see page 60.

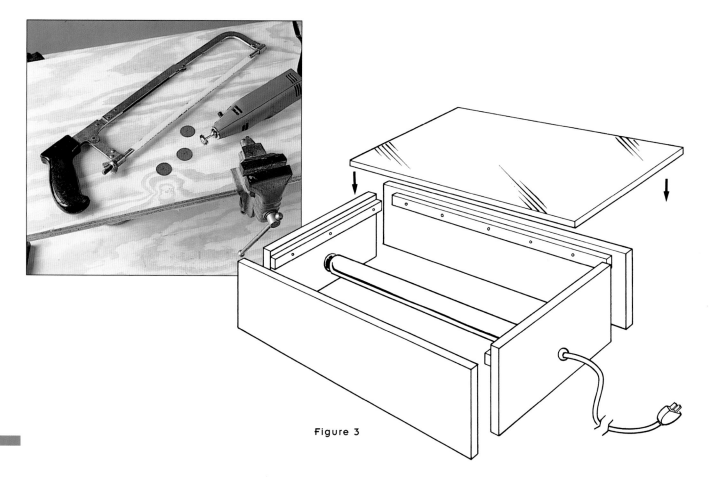

Figure 3

Chapter Five: Scoring and Breaking Glass

Beginners in stained glass sometimes approach their first glass-cutting experience as if they were facing a species of savage beast. If you find yourself imagining fierce and bloody battles with hostile sheets of glass, relax! Scoring and breaking glass isn't terribly difficult. In fact, all it takes is a bit of thought, a comfortable grip on your glass cutter, and some practice.

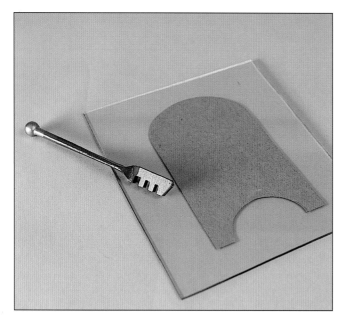

Before we walk you through a practice session, we'd like to explain that you don't actually "cut" glass. First you weaken it by scoring it with a glass cutter, which creates a fissure by separating the glass molecules. You then break the glass by applying pressure along both sides of the score.

We emphasize cutting, grozing, and grinding skills heavily in this book, because the skill with which you perform these processes is always reflected in the finished product. Inaccurate cuts and rough glass edges have a visible effect on the soldered seams of copper foil projects (foil can't be centered properly on glass with angled or uneven edges) and in leaded work, inaccurately cut glass may not assemble properly.

Freehand and Template Scoring

Professional glass cutters use different cutting techniques, but the two most common methods are freehand scoring and template scoring.

In the freehand method, the pattern is placed under the glass; unless the glass is very opaque or dark, the pattern lines show through. The score is then made by guiding the glass cutter along the edge of the visible pattern line. When dark or opaque glass is scored this way, a light box is necessary (see page 32).

While many accomplished artists use the freehand cutting method, we recommend using templates—stiff paper patterns cut to the shape of each piece of glass in a project. The templates are glued to the glass sheets from which you'll cut and serve as guides for your glass cutter. Although making templates may strike you as unnecessarily time consuming, these paper patterns will actually save you time when it comes to grozing and grinding (see page 43) and should leave no question that the pieces you cut will fit!

Holding Your Glass Cutter

The best way to hold your glass cutter is the one with which you're most comfortable. Photo 1 shows the traditional grip on a glass cutter. Photo 2 shows a slightly different version of the same grip. Note that each artist uses the thumb of her free hand to stabilize the cutter and control its path.

Photo 3, in which the cutter is shown at the end of a score, illustrates another grip. The artist uses the forefinger of her free hand to prevent the cutter from dropping off the edge of the sheet. (If you think there's something odd about the cutter angle in this photo, you're right; it's tilted and shouldn't be! You'll discover why in the next section.)

Photo 4 shows a pistol-grip cutter being held in preparation for a curved cut. This cutter is remarkably easy to control, especially if your hands aren't very strong.

During the practice session that's coming up, try out each grip and select the one that feels best. You may want to switch from one grip to another for different types of scores.

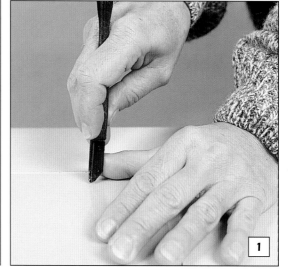

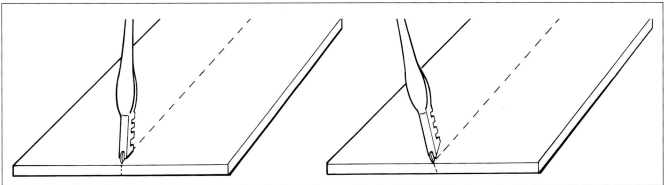

Figure 1

Controlling Your Glass Cutter

Successful glass-cutting depends on several factors; learning to control these factors is a little like learning to drive, but trust us, it's much less terrifying. By the time you've finished this chapter, you'll have learned all the cutting skills you need to make the projects in this book. Read through the following tips before you start:

■ Always keep the cutting wheel perpendicular to the glass; it must never tilt to the left or right. Scores made with a tilted cutter will either break at an angle or fail to break along the entire score (see Figure 1).

■ Glass will only break properly if you start the score at one edge of a piece of glass and continue it right through to another edge.

■ Avoid pulling the handle of the cutter back at an angle toward your body. If the cutter isn't held in an almost upright position, the metal portion at its bottom may scrape the glass behind the

wheel, and you'll also find it difficult, if not impossible, to negotiate curved scores.

■ Apply even pressure to your cutter as you push it across the glass, or the score will be irregular in depth and the glass may not break evenly.

■ Keep the speed at which you move the cutter consistent along the length of the score. The more even the speed you maintain, the more effective the score will be.

■ Some artists prefer to pull the cutter toward themselves instead of pushing the cutter away. We recommend pushing rather than pulling, as pushing leaves the pattern line or template edge visible in front of the cutter wheel. A cutter pulled toward you will often hide the pattern line you're trying to follow. There's one exception to this rule: When making long straight cuts on very large sheets of glass, it's easier to pull than to push.

■ As you score the glass, you should hear a soft hissing sound, not a loud rasp. You should also see a barely visible line in the

cutter's wake. If that line is white and powdery, or if you see glass chips flying as you push the cutter along, you're pressing down too hard. Take a good look at Photo 5. The score on the right was made with far too much pressure; the score on the left is much better.

■ Never score over the same place twice; crossing over a previous score will damage the cutting wheel, and your glass won't break properly, either.

■ The interior lines in patterns represent either the heart of the lead came between two pieces of glass or the thickness of the copper foil wrapped around each piece. (See Chapter 6 for complete descriptions of these lines.) The thickness of these lines isn't an issue when you cut around templates, as your pattern-cutting shears will have sliced away a strip of paper of exactly the right thickness. When cutting freehand, however, you'll need to guide the cutting wheel along the edge of each line, not down its center.

■ After every score you make, lubricate and clean the wheel of your cutter by wiping the wheel across a kerosene- or oil-soaked rag. (Even self-lubricating cutters should be wiped to remove glass chips.) Also remember to clean each piece of glass before scoring it and to brush off your bench—frequently—with your bench brush.

Practice Session: Scoring, Breaking, Grozing, and Grinding

Purchase a few small sheets of ordinary window glass (also known as float glass). It's much less expensive than stained glass and is also very easy to cut. Gather together the tools and materials listed below and set aside an hour or two of uninterrupted time.

Tools and Materials

Several 12"-square (30.5 cm) sheets of float glass

Newspapers

Work board or bench

Glass cleaner

Rags

Safety glasses

Glass cutter

Container with cotton rag and kerosene or sewing-machine oil

Bench brush

Breaking pliers

Running pliers

Grozing pliers

Glass grinder

Enlarged copy of Figure 2

Craft paper

Carbon paper; masking tape, duct tape, or horseshoe nails; straightedge; and pencil—or spray adhesive (see Step 15)

Scissors

Glue stick

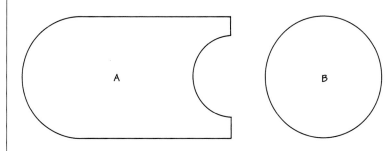

ENLARGE BY 225%   Figure 2

What to Do

1. Spread out a few layers of newspaper on the surface of your work board or bench. (We've eliminated this newspaper from our photos in order to show the glass clearly.) Clean both surfaces of one sheet of float glass. Place the clean glass on the newspaper.

2. Put on your safety glasses, lubricate your cutter, and place the cutter wheel about 1/8" (3 mm) or less from the nearest edge of the glass.

3. Keeping your wrist locked and holding the cutter wheel perpendicular to the glass, push the cutter away from you in a straight line until it's almost at the far edge of the glass. Exert even pressure as you do this and don't allow the cutting wheel to drop off the far edge of the glass (see Photo 3 on page 35).

4. Inspect the score carefully. If it looks white and powdery, you've pressed down too hard on your cutter. Of course the true test of an effective score is whether or not the glass will break cleanly along it. There are several ways to break glass along a straight score; we'll cover them one at a time.

5. Long scores on large sheets can be broken out by hand. Position the scored sheet so the score lies just beyond the edge of the bench. Grip the glass as shown in Figure 3, lift it slightly, and bring it down sharply. The strip you've scored will snap off in your hand.

When making this type of break on very large sheets of glass, use both hands to grip the protruding glass at its edges. To break out the score, lift the sheet slightly and bring it down smartly. Be careful not to drop the section you're holding, or it will drop to the floor below!

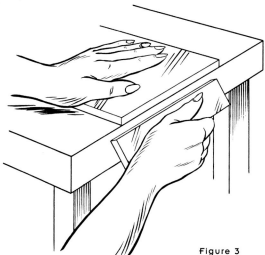

Figure 3

6. To break out long narrow strips, a "bench break," made with breaking pliers, is very effective. Score another straight line about 1" (2.5 cm) from the edge of the float glass. Then position the glass with the score just beyond the edge of the bench. Grip the scored strip with a pair of wide breaking pliers, placing the ends of the jaws parallel to and close to the score but not touching it, and hold the sheet steady with your other hand. Now pull down and out with the pliers (see

Photo 6). The scored strip should break off cleanly.

It's sometimes best on long cuts such as this one to "work" the score gently rather than snapping the scored glass off right away. Begin by placing your breaking pliers at one end of the score and wiggling them slightly, exerting just enough pressure to start what's known as a **run** (a visible deepening of the fissure). Reposition your pliers at the other end of the score, and repeat. Then grip the glass in its center and break out the score.

Practice cutting and breaking out several straight scores in this fashion.

7. Long scores, both curved and straight, may also be broken out with running pliers. Score one more straight line on a full sheet of float glass. This time, position a pair of running pliers directly over the score, with the concave jaw on top and the guide mark directly above the score (see Photo 7 on the next page). Place the fingers or palm of your free hand midway along the score. By exerting slight pressure here, you'll prevent the run from veering away from the score and cracking the glass. To start the run, squeeze the plier handles together gently. Now reposition the pliers at the other end of the score and squeeze gently again. As the second run meets the first, the strip should break off cleanly.

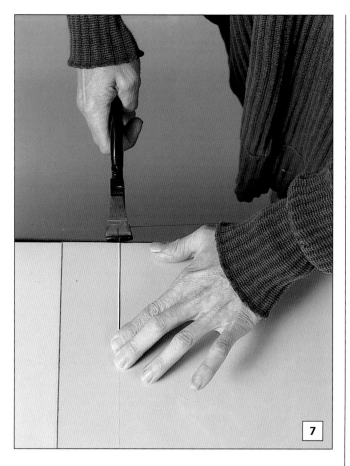

8. On pieces of glass small enough to control with your hands, a "thumb break" is sometimes easiest. Score a straight line and grip the glass as shown in Photo 8. Place your thumbs close to the score, grip the glass firmly, and pull down and apart (See Photo 9). If the glass resists, refer to "Tech Tip: Tapping" on page 42.

Look closely at the cut edges of each piece. If they aren't perpendicular to the glass surface, you probably tilted your cutter to the left or right. Are the edges chipped and ragged? You may have varied the pressure on your cutter or stopped and started the cut instead of pushing the cutter along in one fluid motion. Don't worry if the edge is rough; you'll soon learn how to groze and/or grind it to shape.

Practice the thumb break on several straight scores.

9. Score another straight line on a relatively narrow piece of glass. This time, use two pairs of narrow-jawed breaking pliers to break out the score, holding them as shown in Photo 10 and pulling down and apart on them. Try this breaking method on several scores.

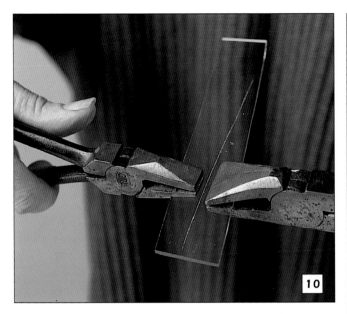

10. Sometimes it's easiest to break out a score by using one hand and a pair of breaking pliers, usually on very small pieces with straight scores (see Photo 11). Practice this breaking method until you're comfortable with it.

11. When you score straight lines, using a cutting square (available through stained glass suppliers) or handmade jig as a cutter guide can be very helpful (see Photo 12). Hold the square in place with one hand as you guide the cutter with the other. Whether you're cutting freehand over a pattern or are using a template, remember to position the cutting wheel—not the straightedge—over the line you wish to cut.

For instructions on building two helpful implements for making straight cuts, turn to page 30.

12. Curved lines (see Photo 13 on the next page) are scored in almost the same way as straight ones, but be sure to position the glass so you can follow through with the score in one

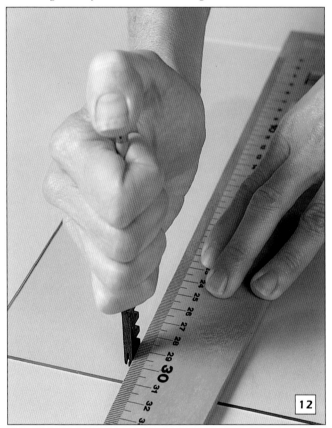

fluid motion. If you forget to do this, you may find that you have to stop the score in order to reposition your body—never a good idea!

Before making this score, go through the motions a few times without letting the cutting wheel touch the glass. (Professional glass cutters often act out a cut this way before they actually execute it.) By moving your whole torso and holding your elbow to your side, you should be able to follow the score through to its completion without stopping your cutter. Complete the actual score now (see Photo 14 on the next page).

13. The most effective way to break out a gently curved score is by using running pliers (see Step 7). If you don't own a pair of these pliers, use breaking pliers, a thumb break, and/or tapping. Practice breaking out several gently arced scores.

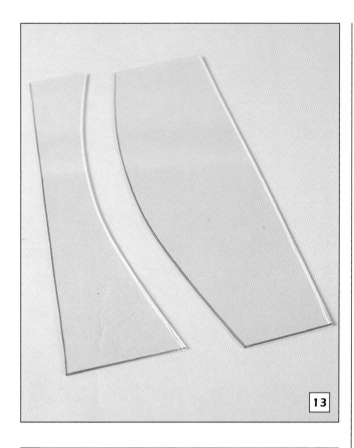

13

14

14. Next, try a few wavy scores (see Photo 15). You'll find that running pliers also work well on these.

15. In the next few steps, you'll learn how to make and use templates. On a flat table or your work surface, spread out a sheet of craft paper that is somewhat larger than your enlarged copy of patterns A and B. Then use one of the following two methods to make templates:

Method One: Place a sheet of carbon paper, face down, on top of the craft paper. Cover the carbon paper with the copy of the patterns. Tape or nail all three sheets down so they

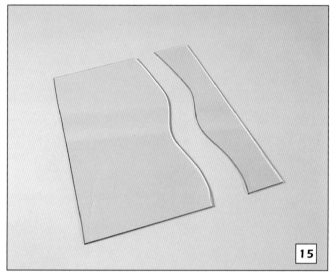

15

won't shift as you work and trace over the pattern lines, using a straightedge and pencil. Peel away the tape and separate the sheets of paper.

Method Two: Glue the pattern copy to the craft paper with permanent spray adhesive. Be sure to smooth away any wrinkles as you do this.

16. Using a pair of scissors, cut out the shapes of templates A and B from the craft paper. (When you cut templates for actual projects, you'll use pattern shears instead.) Note that if you glued your pattern to the craft paper, you'll be cutting through both sheets.

17. Cut a small piece of float glass, at least 1/2" (1.3 cm) larger on all sides than template A. Cutting small blanks in this fashion serves several purposes. First, it prevents waste; if you slip up while breaking out a score, you'll only destroy the blank, not an entire sheet! Second, the border of glass surrounding the template will give your pliers or hands something to grip when it's time to break out the scores. Don't try to make this border any smaller; breaking off very narrow pieces of glass is difficult. Third, if you make an inaccurate cut and your blank is large enough, you may be able to reposition your template on the same blank rather than having to use an entirely new piece of glass.

18. Use a glue stick to affix template A to the blank. In Figure 4, the cuts you'll need to make are numbered in consecutive order. Score and break out Line 1 first.

Now take a look at Line 4. This cut would be extremely difficult to break out accurately at this stage; the glass would be likely to crack along lines A or B. To break out semicircles like this one, you'll need to score and break out, one at a time, two or more scallops (Lines 2 and 3), removing glass gradually to relieve the pressure at Line 4.

Position your glass blank so that you'll be able to complete each cut in one fluid motion (see Photo 16). Score and break out Lines 2, 3, and 4 (see Photo 17). Don't worry if the edge of the break at Line 4 isn't completely even. Unwanted bits of remaining glass may be grozed or ground away later.

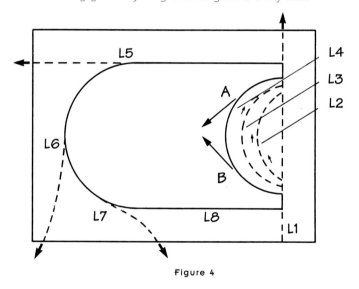

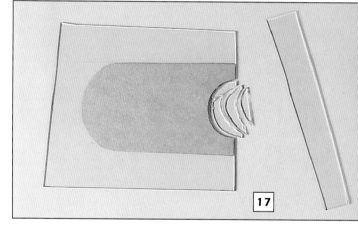

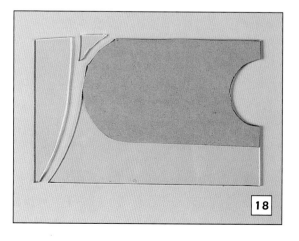

Figure 4

19. Score and break out Line 5. Note that if Lines 5 and 8 had been scored and broken out before Line 4, the glass around the semicircle would have been weakened considerably and would have been much more likely to snap off.

20. To score and break the convex semicircle, you'll use a technique similar to that used in Step 18, but this time, you'll score and break out the semicircle in sections. Start by scoring and breaking out Line 6 (see Photo 18). Note that when we broke this line out, the glass cracked. This didn't concern us, as the break was on the waste section of glass. Score and break Line 7 next.

21. Finally score and break out Line 8 (see Photo 19). Set aside the template-covered piece of glass. In a few minutes, you'll learn how to groze and grind its rough edges.

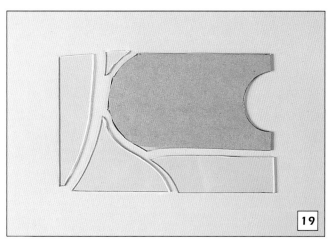

22. Glue template B to another blank of glass, leaving at least 1/2" (1.3 cm) of glass around the perimeter.

23. Although commercial circle-cutting tools are available, cutting circles by hand is not as difficult as you might think. First study Figure 5. As you can see, you'll score and break out the circle gradually rather than by trying to score the entire circle at one time. Score and break out Lines 1, 2, 3, and 4, one at a time (see Photo 20) and set the template-covered circle aside.

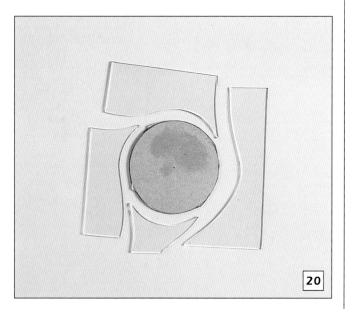

24. Time for your first pat on the back! Believe it or not, with the skills you've learned and a bit more practice, you'll be able to cut glass for hundreds of beautiful projects.

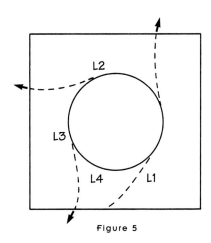

Figure 5

TECH TIP

TAPPING

If you've wondered why a traditional glass cutter has a ball shape at the end of its handle, here's the answer: The ball is used to tap along the underside of resistant scores. Hold the glass and cutter as shown in Photo 21, making sure that you support both pieces of glass so that you can catch them as the break occurs.

Tap the ball, sharply but not hard, directly underneath the score at either end. (Never start tapping in the middle of the score.) You should see a run starting to develop; this is a deepening of the fissure created by scoring the glass. Continue to tap in this fashion, working from one end of the score toward the other end, until the glass breaks apart or is sufficiently weakened to break out with pliers. Tapping does tend to create chipped or jagged edges along the break, so be prepared to groze or grind the finished pieces.

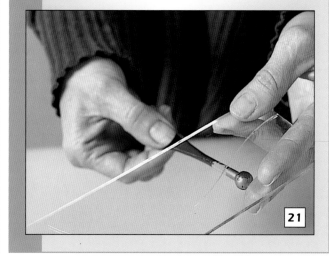

25. Grozing—carefully nibbling away unwanted glass—is done with grozing pliers (see Photo 22). These pliers may be used in a number of ways, so do experiment with them. Using your cut glass circle for practice, gently nibble at the protruding glass edges by rolling the corners of the jaws or their flat edges down and over the sections you want to remove. Try rolling them up and over the glass, too. Don't squeeze hard on the plier handles. Your goal is make the glass edge match the edge of the template by removing tiny chips of glass, not chunks! To control the plier jaws, place your index finger between the handles. Grozing won't yield perfectly smooth edges, but it will remove obvious bits of excess glass.

26. If you've never operated a glass grinder before, read the manufacturer's operating and care instructions carefully before you start. Also refer to page 31 for a description of this tool's functions.

Put on your safety glasses, turn the grinder on, and place the template-covered glass on its upper surface, with the template facing up. Holding the glass firmly, slide it toward the spinning grinder bit until the protruding edge of the glass touches the bit (see Photo 23). Press the glass firmly against the bit so it doesn't dance about and chip, moving it back and forth until the edge of the glass has been ground to match the edge of the template. Placing a small block of wood between the edge of the glass and your fingers will help you control small pieces that are difficult to grasp, will protect your fingers, and will help to prevent the template from sliding out of position.

Do be careful not to press too hard, or the grinder bit will eat away too much glass too quickly, and you may find that the

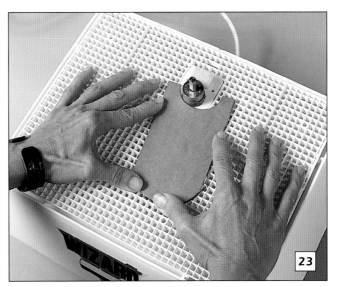

glass gets trapped on the bit. Also take care not to round off corners or points.

Occasionally, you may need to grind commercial bevels, jewels, and globs, either to make them fit your pattern or to rough up their edges so that copper foil will adhere well. Before grinding bevels, cover their polished surfaces, which are more susceptible to scratching than the surfaces of sheet glass, with masking tape or adhesive-backed plastic.

Remember our reference to templates as time-savers? If you had cut your glass using the freehand method, you would lose a great deal of time at the grinding stage because you'd be toting the cut piece back and forth to your pattern in order to identify the edges in need of work. To make this task somewhat easier, set the cut piece on the pattern and use a waterproof marker to darken any edges that protrude beyond the pattern lines. Unfortunately, you may find yourself repeating this step several times, as even waterproof marker ink tends to be washed away by the water-lubricated grinder bit.

Congratulations! You've just learned how to cut, groze, and grind glass.

Following are a few more tips to help you as you cut glass for your projects:

■ Small to medium sheets of glass may be broken by positioning the score over one edge of a straightedge or a glass cutter and pressing down on opposite sides of the glass (see Figure 6).

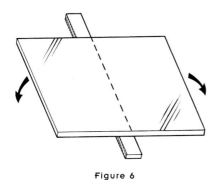

Figure 6

■ Always score art glass on its smoother or shinier side. Feel the glass surfaces for bumps, ripples, or striations. If you can't distinguish the smoother side this way, hold the sheet up to reflect strong light so that textures will be visible. If you're still uncertain, make a couple of experimental cuts on a scrap of the same type of glass. Once you've identified the cutting surface, be sure that every piece you cut from it is scored on the same side!

■ Typically, the smooth glass surfaces (and beveled edges of jewels) face outward when a panel is displayed. If you'd rather display the textured surfaces of sheet glass in your panel, flip your templates over before affixing them to the glass.

■ On glass that is not consistent in thickness, score and break from the thicker toward the thinner edge.

■ Waste not, want not! Position your templates (or, if you're scoring freehand, your full pattern) to take advantage of the glass. Align straight edges of the templates, for example, along a straight edge of the glass from which you're cutting.

■ Break each score line right after you make it; then score the next line.

■ To help prevent sharp tips from cracking off as you break concave score lines, complete the concave cuts before scoring and breaking the lines that meet them.

■ Score and break more difficult cuts and longer lines before easier and shorter ones.

■ When scoring glass that is heavily textured or bubbled, position your templates to avoid obstructions. When this is impossible, and if your cutter comes to a halt mid-score, don't force it through the obstruction. Lift it up and reposition it just a slight distance away to continue the score. Try tapping scores such as these to force a run through the obstruction.

■ Always cut mirrored glass on the glass side, not on the silvered side.

■ The edges of cut glass sometimes have paper-thin, extremely sharp, and nearly invisible protrusions on them. To dull these edges for safe handling, scrape a piece of scrap glass or the edge of your grozing pliers against both the top and bottom of the cut edge.

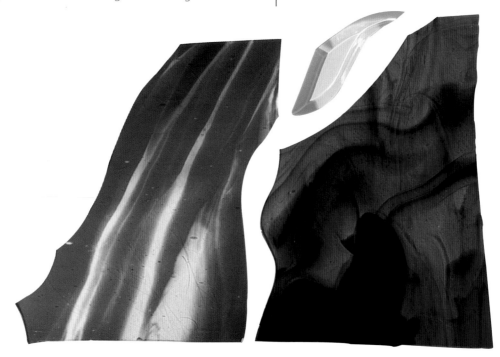

Chapter Six: Patterns and Templates

In this chapter, you'll learn how to size and copy patterns and create cutting templates. In addition, you'll make templates and cut glass for your first copper foil or leaded glass panel; turn to pages 50 and 59 to see photos of these panels.

Commercial Patterns

Until you've had some experience cutting glass and working with copper foil and leaded glass projects, we suggest that you use commercially available patterns rather than trying to create your own. Start with a few of the patterns in this book; they've all been designed specifically for beginners and working with them will allow you to practice both basic assembly techniques and more sophisticated variations such as foil overlays. Working with commercial patterns will also teach you some of the limitations that cutting glass can present, an important step toward learning to design patterns of your own.

When you're ready to start exploring other patterns, browse through the pattern books available at your local stained glass shop. Ask for addresses of mail-order pattern suppliers, too. Don't forget your public library; you may very well find pattern books on its shelves. Hundreds of commercial patterns are available in a huge array of styles, shapes, and sizes.

Exterior Pattern Lines

Before you use a pattern to cut glass to size, you should understand how patterns are sized. Take a good look at Figure 1. Although purchased patterns may not depict them, there are three sets of exterior border lines to consider.

■The **perimeter line** represents the outer edge of the border came on the completed panel. These dimensions are only important when you plan to insert your panel into another frame such as a window or door; they must be calculated exactly so the panel will fit into this second frame with a little play.

■The **exterior cut line** represents the outer edges of the exterior glass pieces in the panel. These edges will be tucked into and hidden by the border came.

■The **sight line** describes the visual opening of the panel—the glass you'll be able to see when the border came or, in architectural installations, the architectural framing, is in place. In the case on non-installed panels, the distance between the cut line and sight line will depend on the width of the flange on the border came you're using. When you use 1/4" (6 mm) zinc came, for example, this distance will be 1/16" (1.5 mm).

Determining Border-Line Placement

Most patterns include only the cut lines, but adding perimeter and sight lines is an easy matter. To determine the placement of perimeter lines (always the first step when designing for architectural installations and when leading up a panel), cut a scrap of the border came you intend to use and a scrap of glass with one straight edge. Position the straight edge of the glass along the inside edge of the cut line on your pattern. Slip the came scrap over the edge of the glass, press the glass against the came's heart, and mark the position of the came's outer edge onto the pattern (see Photo 1). Repeat to make one or two more marks at different positions; then use a pencil and straightedge to create the perimeter line by joining

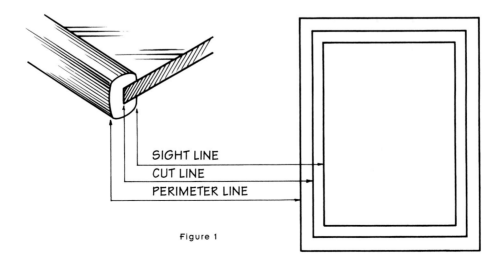

SIGHT LINE
CUT LINE
PERIMETER LINE

Figure 1

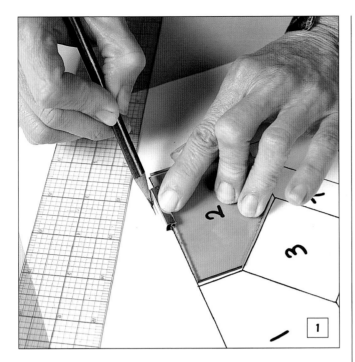

these marks. This line should run exactly parallel to the cut line. Include the perimeter line on all four sides of the pattern.

To determine the sight line, use the same technique to mark the inner edge of the border came onto your pattern. You may also determine the position of these lines mathematically by referring to the came dimensions, which are often provided by the manufacturer.

Interior Pattern Lines

Interior pattern lines define the shapes of the glass pieces. Their thickness is important because the glass pieces must be cut to allow enough space between them to accommodate either the heart of the lead came or the foil on the glass edges (see "Pattern Shears" on page 28).

In many commercial patterns, including the ones in this book, pattern lines are not drawn to any particular width. Pattern shears will determine the line width for you, so always be sure you're using the correct set of pattern shears when you cut templates!

We recommend using shears, but if you'd rather cut your glass freehand, you'll need to establish the correct pattern-line width by drawing over the pattern lines with a medium-point (for leaded panels) or a fine-point (for copper foil projects) felt-tip marker.

Copying and Enlarging Patterns

You'll need three copies of any pattern you intend to use: one to file away for future use; one (full size) from which to make templates; and one (also full size) on which to assemble your project. Unless the original pattern is drawn to full size, you'll need to enlarge or reduce it.

The best way to enlarge or reduce a pattern is to use the services of a blueprint shop. First, make two photocopies or clear carbon tracings of the original pattern and file one away for future reference. Then take the other to the blueprint shop and have two full-size blueprints made.

If your community lacks a blueprint shop, head for a photocopy shop instead. The personnel there should be able to help you create full-size patterns. Do double-check finished pattern sizes; photocopiers sometimes distort patterns slightly.

You may also size patterns by using a grid. Draw a grid of 1/2" (1.3 cm) squares over a copy of the original pattern. On a sheet of paper that is at least 4" (10.2 cm) longer and wider than the full-size pattern will be, draw a second grid containing the same number of squares, but make each square larger (or smaller) than the ones in your pattern grid. Then, in each square of the blank grid, draw the contents of the equivalent box in the pattern grid. While this enlargement technique can be tedious, it's very effective.

Cutting the Glass for Your First Project

The instructions that follow will walk you through cutting the glass pieces for your first copper foil or leaded glass panel. Gather the tools and materials listed below and select your glass before you begin.

Tools and Materials

Basic tool set
Glass of your choice
2 enlarged copies of Figure 2 (on page 48)
Carbon paper; masking tape, duct tape, or horseshoe nails;
    straightedge; and pencil—or spray adhesive
Craft paper
Waterproof marker and paint pen
Glue stick
Scrub brush or toothbrush
Rags

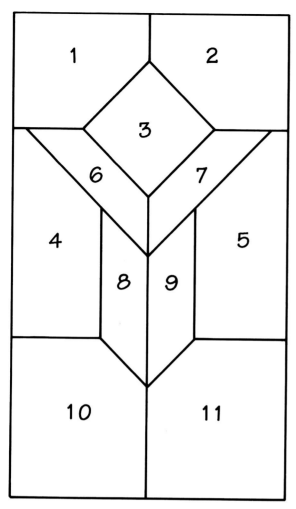

Figure 2 Enlarge 200%

What to Do

1. To help you keep track of the pieces of glass you cut, number each section on both patterns. This project has very few glass pieces, but when you work with larger, more complex patterns or with pieces that are similar in shape, designing and using a color and/or position coding system is also help-

ful. In a pattern depicting many flowers, for example, you might code the leaf shapes as L1, L2 , L3, etc. and the petal shapes as P1, P2, and so on.

To indicate which way you'd like the colors and textures of the glass to run, mark arrows on any pattern sections that you plan to cut from opals or from glasses with directional patterns in them.

2. Transfer one of the two patterns to a piece of craft paper, following the instructions on page 40 (see Photo 2).

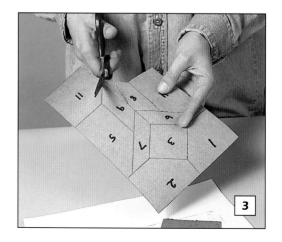

3. Using ordinary scissors or a craft knife and straightedge, cut along the exterior cut lines of the craft-paper pattern. Then, using the appropriate pattern shears (you'll need to decide now whether to make a copper foil panel or a leaded glass panel), cut out the various pattern pieces. Be careful to center the shears over the pattern lines (see Photo 3).

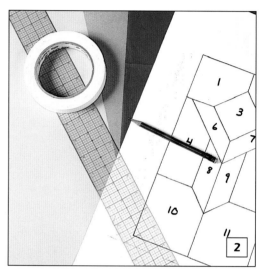

4. Place your selected glass sheets on your work surface, with their smooth (or shinier) surfaces facing up. Then experiment with the templates by positioning them loosely on the sheets (see Photo 4), keeping the following goals in mind:

■ Ideally, adjoining pieces cut from the same color and type of glass should be cut so that streaks of color and textures run in a consistent manner, from one piece up to the next, for example. In geometric designs such this one, keep the "grain" running consistently. Avoid cutting adjoining pieces from entirely different sections of the same sheet of opaque glass, as the variations in color may be quite noticeable.

■ Preventing waste is always a good idea, but you'll need to leave enough space around each template to give your breaking pliers (or hands) something to grip when breaking out the scores.

■ Position the templates so that two or three can be cut from a single blank.

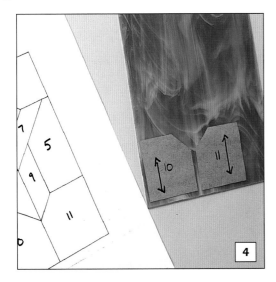

5. After all the templates have been positioned, cut blanks in the form of strips. Strips should hold two or three templates apiece, with room to spare. Next, use a glue stick to affix two or three templates to the surface of one blank. Cut these pieces of glass, and then glue down two or three more templates, repeating this sequence until all pieces have been cut.

6. Groze and grind the edges of each cut piece until these edges are even with the template edges.

7. Remove the templates by soaking the pieces of glass in water for a few minutes. Scrub any remaining glue from the glass (an old toothbrush works well), and dry the glass well. If your pattern

TECH TIP

GLUING TEMPLATES TO GLASS

Avoid gluing down all your templates at the same time. If you accidentally crack a blank while you're cutting and need to rearrange the templates on other blanks in order to make room for the one you need to recut, you won't have to soak off templates that have been glued in place for hours. Just peel up the template from the cracked glass (a dip in water will loosen semi-hardened glue), and glue it onto another blank or, if there's room, in a different position on the old blank.

is complex, symmetrical, or has two or more pieces similar in shape, use a waterproof marker or paint pen to mark each template code onto the glass itself. Double-check the pieces by placing them on the assembly pattern (see Photo 5), keeping in mind that the pieces shouldn't touch each other. The slight space around every piece will allow for the heart of the lead or the solder that will adhere to the foiled edges. If any pieces fail to match their pattern outlines, groze and grind them as needed—or cut new pieces.

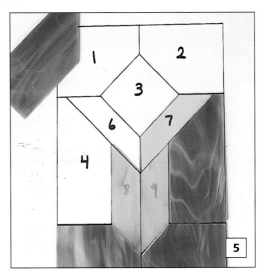

8. To construct a copper foil panel, turn to Chapter 7, "Working with Copper Foil." To asemble a leaded glass panel, turn to Chapter 8, "Working with Lead Came."

Chapter Seven: Working with Copper Foil

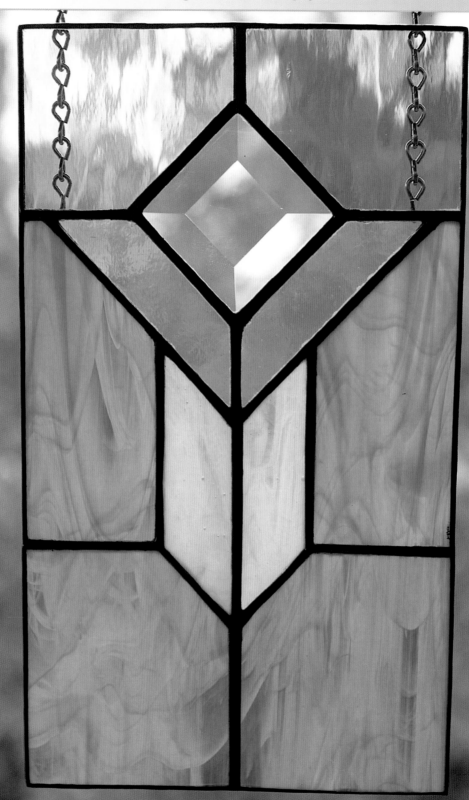

A technique similar to contemporary copper foil construction was first practiced during the late 1800s to make lamp shades. Because lead came simply wasn't pliable enough to shape to the curved Art Nouveau pattern pieces of the time, artists (among them the famed Tiffany), shaped flexible copper or brass channeling around each cut piece of glass to serve as a base for soldering.

Copper foil projects are extremely popular with beginning stained glass enthusiasts and experts alike, and they're certainly an excellent place to start if you've never worked with glass before. In this chapter, you'll learn how to assemble your cut pieces of glass into a finished copper foil panel.

Tools and Materials

Basic tool set

Enlarged copy of Figure 2 (on page 48)

Cut glass pieces (see Chapter 6)

1 roll of 7/32"-wide (5.4 mm) copper foil

Masking tape or horseshoe nails

2 lath strips, each at least 12" (30.5 cm) long

3/4" (1.9 cm) brads

Flux and flux brushes

50/50 or 60/40 solder

Fine-grade steel wool

Medium-gauge pretinned copper wire

Rags

Newspapers

Whiting, patching plaster, or plaster of paris

Scrub brush

Toothbrush

Dishwashing detergent

Baking soda

Patina (optional)

Finishing compound or car wax (optional)

What to Do

Foiling

The solder you apply to your project will hold the pieces together and provide a strong framework for them. Because solder will not adhere to glass, you must provide a base for it by wrapping copper foil around the edges of each piece of glass.

1. Assemble your pieces of cut glass, tools, and supplies. Be sure that your hands and all pieces of glass are clean.

2. Open the package of copper foil. Unwind, tear off, and discard one coil. Unwind another few inches of foil and peel back about 1/2" (1.3 cm) of the paper backing on it.

3. Holding a piece of glass in one hand and starting anywhere on an edge that will face the interior of the assembled panel, center the edge of the glass on the adhesive surface of the foil and press the foil flat against the edge of the glass (see Photo 1). Starting and ending a foil wrap on an exterior edge will make it difficult to form a smooth solder border for your panel.

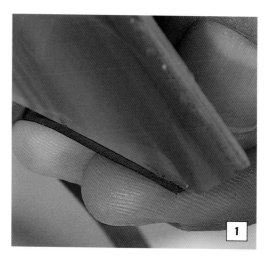

4. Continue to wrap the foil around the edge of the glass, peeling back the adhesive strip a little at a time and pressing the foil against the glass edge with one finger. Be careful to keep the foil centered on the glass edges, especially as you work around corners (see Photo 2).

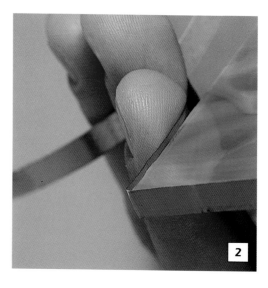

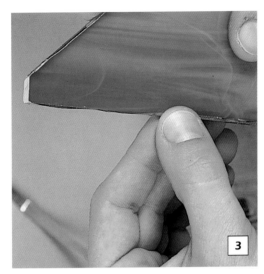

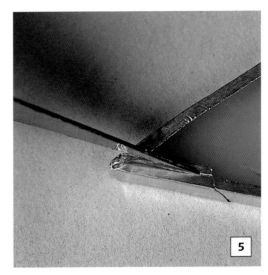

5. When you reach the point at which you started, cover the previously applied foil by about 1/4" (6 mm), tear or cut off the foil at that point, and press the end firmly in place. Then press the narrow margins of foil against both flat surfaces of the glass (see Photo 3). An equal margin of foil should wrap around each surface. To press down the margins at sharp corners or curves, overlap them by folding one over the other (see Photo 4).

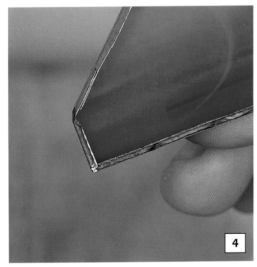

6. Inspect the foiled glass carefully. If you've accidentally wrapped the foil unevenly, you'll see that the foil margin on one surface is wider than the margin on the opposite surface. Uneven margins are most likely to occur at corners, at the point where the foil overlaps itself, and on glass with an undulating surface texture. If the margins are uneven at a corner or where one end of the foil overlaps the other, trim the offending foil with a craft knife (see Photo 5) and peel it

away. If the margins are uneven along the edges and can't be trimmed effectively, peel away the foil, reclean the glass, and rewrap with new foil.

7. Using a burnisher of any type, firmly rub the foil down to secure it onto the edges and both surfaces of the glass (see Photo 6).

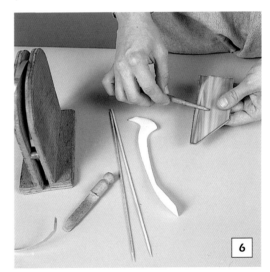

8. Repeat Steps 3 through 7 to foil, burnish, and trim all the glass pieces.

9. Brush off your work surface. Set your assembly pattern on it, tacking down the corners with masking tape or horseshoe nails.

10. To keep the corners of this rectangular project at perfect right angles during assembly, you must construct a jig on top of the pattern (see Photo 7). Align the interior edges of the two lath strips with the exterior cut lines on the pattern. Using a square, check to see that the strips form a perfect 90° angle. Then nail

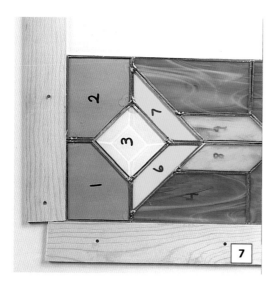

them to your work board. Double-check the angle at the juncture; to make minor adjustments, hammer gently on the outer edge of either strip. (If you're right-handed, it seems natural to build this L-shaped jig in the lower left-hand corner of your pattern.)

11. Arrange the foiled glass on the pattern, keeping in mind that there should be some play between the pieces; don't jam them together! Using your right angle again, make sure that all corners are square and that all edge pieces are aligned with the exterior cut lines; if they aren't even, your soldered border won't be even.

Tack-Soldering

Tack-soldering serves to attach the pieces to one another so they won't shift as you create solder beads (see Photo 7). Plug in your iron and allow it to heat. Put on your safety glasses. Before you begin Step 12, read "Tech Tip: Soldering."

12. Starting with a seam at the top of the project and working downward, dab a small amount of liquid flux at any point along the seam between two pieces of glass. If you're right-handed, start at the upper left-hand corner and work downward and to the right so you won't be dragging your hands or soldering-iron cord through the flux.

13. Unwind a few inches of solder from the solder spool and, gripping the spool in one hand, position the end of the solder wire just above the fluxed seam. Holding your soldering iron in the other hand, touch the hot tip to the end of the solder wire and press the molten solder onto the foil. Hold down the iron just long enough to allow the solder to adhere to the seam—one sec-

SOLDERING

—Every time you finish soldering a seam, wipe the tip of your hot iron on a damp rag or natural-fiber sponge. A clean tip transfers heat more effectively.

—Whenever your soldering iron won't be in use for periods longer than 15 minutes, unplug it.

—While adjustable-temperature soldering irons are more versatile than those which maintain a constant temperature, they will need periodic adjustment. If, for example, your solder melts into a shape that resembles a miniature Mt. Everest, complete with peaks, you've either forgotten to flux the foil (see Step 12), or your iron is too cold—turn the temperature control up!

—Soldering irons are extremely hot. Holding the tip down too long on a copper foil seam may cause the glass to crack (narrow pieces are especially vulnerable) or the foil to lift from the glass. Use a light touch when you solder!

—Your solder will tell you when you've forgotten to apply flux, when you need to apply more, or when the copper foil has oxidized — it won't flow properly. Instead, you'll end up with ugly solder lumps. To clean oxidized copper foil wrapped on glass, wipe it well with fine-grade steel wool.

—Avoid inhaling flux fumes when soldering; they're toxic.

ond or less. The solder will hold the two foiled pieces of glass together at that point.

14. Repeat Step 13 to tack all the foiled pieces together. To speed up this process, apply dabs of flux to several seams, tack those seams with solder, and then move on to flux and solder a few more seams.

Soldering Seams

Now you're ready to shape what are known as **beads** (slightly rounded lines of solder) over the tacked seams. Keep in mind that if you'd like to include a zinc or lead border on this panel, instead of the soldered border that we'll teach you how to make, you mustn't run your solder beads all the way to the outer edges of the panel, or you won't be able to fit the border came over the seams. For instructions on installing a zinc or lead came border, see Chapter 8.

15. Brush a small amount of liquid flux along the full length of a tacked seam that lies in the upper portion of the project. Then read the next two steps carefully before you continue!

16. Think of soldering seams as a two-step process: First, you'll apply the correct amount of solder all along the seam. Then you'll smooth out the seam by going back over it with your iron.

Hold your iron and the spool of solder over a fluxed seam, about 1/8" (3 mm) below the project's upper edge. With the tip of the iron, pick up about 1/4" (6 mm) of the solder wire and dab it onto the seam, pressing the iron down just long enough to allow the solder to flow over it. Then lift the iron straight up, without dragging it forward or back, and move it and the solder to the next portion of exposed foil on the seam. Melt another 1/4" of the solder wire onto the seam, continuing in this fashion until you get close to the end of the seam (see Photos 8 and 9). Try to maintain a steady rhythm and apply a consistent amount of solder in consecutive applications, leaving no foil visible. We recommend 50/50 solder for this process because it cools more slowly than 60/40 and won't form ridges as quickly.

Knowing how much solder to apply to a given width of copper foil takes some practice. Too little solder, and the bead will be too flat. Just add more. Too much solder, and the bead won't smooth out, but will jiggle around like gelatin. To remove excess solder, flick it away with the tip of your iron. (If the panel is small and completely assembled, enlist the help of gravity by lifting and tilting it as you do this.) Do be careful;

flying bits of hot solder can burn you.

17. At this stage, you'll probably see ridges in the soldered seam, where the solder has cooled and hardened between applications. To make the bead smooth, bring the iron tip back to the start of the seam. Insert the corner of the tip into

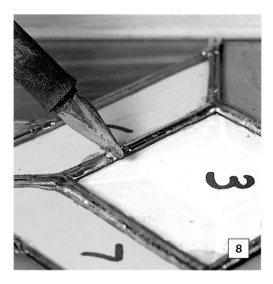

the bead until the solder melts. Lift the iron straight up and reinsert it at the end of this molten area. Lift the iron again and reinsert it at the end of this next molten area. Continue in this manner all the way down the seam (see Photos 10 and 11). Don't brush, prod, or manipulate the solder in any way; the liquid solder will seek its own level and will form a beautiful, smooth bead.

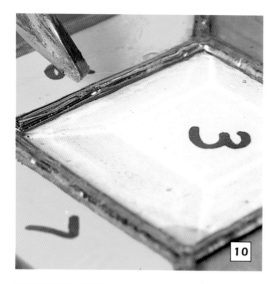

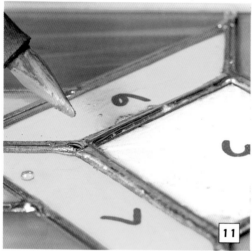

You can only proceed at the correct speed! Work too quickly, and the solder won't melt—you'll end up with ridges along the seam. Go too slowly, and the solder will bleed through to the other side of the panel. (You'll deal with these leaks after you turn the panel over.) You may rework seams as often as you like, but do add flux each time and don't allow the glass to get too hot, or it will crack.

When you're smoothing a bead and come to an intersection where another bead meets it, as you approach the juncture, quickly reheat about 1/2" (1.3 cm) of the entering bead and then continue along the bead you were smoothing. The two molten beads should blend at their meeting point.

Now, repeat Steps 16 and 17 to solder all the seams on this side of the panel.

18. Slide the panel from the jig and, using a cotton rag, wipe as much flux from it as possible. Then turn it over and solder the seams on the other side. Keep an eye out for solder that has leaked through from the other side as you do this; remelt this solder as you apply more to the seam. When you're finished, check all the seams on both sides of the panel, and rework as necessary.

Cold-Soldered Borders

While larger panels require a more stable border of zinc or lead came, small projects may be finished by cold-soldering a bead around the outer edges. This is an especially good technique for pieces with irregularly shaped edges.

19. Flux and tin both the edges and margins along all four exterior edges of the panel. (For instructions on tinning, see "Tech Tip: Running a Bead" on page 56.) No copper foil should be visible when you're finished. Using two heavy objects or a homemade jig (two boards nailed upright with a gap just wide enough to hold the panel between them), brace the project in a vertical position. Its upper edge must be parallel to the ground or the force of gravity will cause the molten solder to flow unevenly.

20. Reapply flux to the tinned upper edge and margins of the foil. Position the solder spool as shown in Photo 12, with the end of the wire bent into a snake shape up and over the edge of the panel.

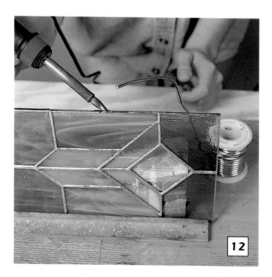

21. To form the border bead, apply solder as you would when making a normal surface bead, moving the iron with small up-and-down motions from the border to the solder wire and back. To prevent the foil edges from lifting away

R U N N I N G   A   B E A D

Another way to solder seams, one which works especially well with quick-melting 60/40 solder, is to run the bead in a single fluid motion rather than melting globs of solder along the seam. Before doing this, you must **tin** (apply a thin, flat coat of solder to) the seams and allow them to cool. Tinned seams serve as a base for the solder bead, helping the solder to flow quickly and evenly.

To best use this technique, tin the foil on the edges of every piece of glass before you assemble the panel. Flux the foil first. Then take a small dab of 50/50 solder onto the tip of the iron and wipe the flat tip along the foiled edge. Repeat until all glass edges have been tinned. Next, arrange the pieces on the pattern, tack them together, and tin all surface seams. (A tinned seam is shown in Photo 13.) We recommend 50/50 solder for tinning because it melts at a higher temperature than 60/40 solder and will prevent your 60/40 beading solder from leaking through to the other side of the panel.

Reflux the tinned seams. Unwind a length of 60/40 solder and position the tip of the soldering iron at the top of the seam; hold the end of the solder wire nearby. Starting a short distance from one end of a seam, move the solder and the tip of the iron right along the seam in a single motion, feeding the solder into the iron and melting it onto the seam as you draw the iron along. If too much solder appears to be melting, pull the solder wire away for a moment and continue to run the iron along the seam; it will pull any excess solder along with it (see Photos 14 and 15).

Reflux the seams and smooth each bead by drawing the corner of the iron steadily along it from one end to the other.

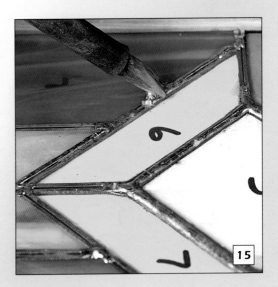

from the glass, cool and clean your iron frequently by wiping it on the sponge or rag. If your iron has a temperature control, turn the heat down. (A relatively cool iron will still pick up solder and carry it the short distance to the panel's edge.)

Occasionally, you may find that molten solder drips down the front or back of your project. Because the solder cools rapidly as it falls, you can usually lift it away easily by hand.

The finished bead should be slightly rounded over the entire surface of the foil. Think of what you're doing as creating a rounded U-shaped solder "came" as a border for your project.

To cold-solder borders around the edges of projects that aren't flat or that don't have straight edges, you may need to hold the project with one hand while you solder with the other. Be sure not to grip the project with your bare hand! Use a rag or heavy gloves to protect your fingers, as the glass can become quite hot, and dripping solder may scald you.

22. Repeat Steps 20 and 21 to cold-solder the remaining three edges of your project. When you're finished, check the solder wherever the border meets a seam and, if necessary, reheat the solder to blend it at these points.

Hooks

Take a look at the photo of the finished panel on page 50. The chains on this panel are attached to hooks that are soldered to the seams running from the corners of the bevel. (If the hooks were soldered to the cold-soldered border, the weight of the panel would rip the border away.)

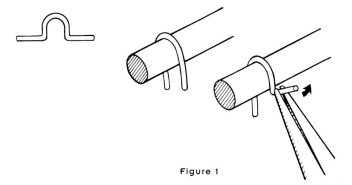

Figure 1

23. Using any round object, bend a short length of medium-gauge, pretinned copper wire as shown in Figure 1. Position the panel face down. Flux the seam where you want the hook to rest. Grasp the U-shaped portion of the hook with pliers and flux the hook's legs. Holding the hook perfectly still against the seam, solder the legs into the seam. If the hook is jostled before the solder cools, it won't be attached firmly.

Hooks this shape may also be soldered to the top of zinc border came on larger panels, but use brazing rod or heavy-gauge wire when making hooks for heavier panels. More on hooks later!

Cleaning

Flux residues must be removed from your project as soon as you've finished soldering, as the acidic flux may haze the glass.

24. To remove liquid flux, fill a container with a mixture of dishwashing liquid, bicarbonate of soda (baking soda), and water. Place the panel in a large sink, a dish pan, or a bathtub and, using a clean rag and scrub brush, scrub the panel thoroughly with the detergent mixture. (Commercial flux removers are available, but this homemade cleaner will work well.) You'll find that a toothbrush is useful for cleaning tough spots along the seams.

If you've chosen to use a paste flux, here's how to remove it. Set the panel on several layers of newspaper and sprinkle it liberally with whiting, patching plaster, or plaster of paris. Allow the powder to sit for a few minutes. Then use a dry scrub brush to work the powder over the glass and along the seams. As you do this, the powder will absorb all the flux. Turn the panel over, repeat, and brush away any excess powder. Wipe the project with a clean dry rag and skip the rinsing and drying stage of the next step.

25. Rinse the project thoroughly and dry with a clean rag. Polish the seams with a piece of fine-grade steel wool; this will remove oxidation as well as any oozing adhesive released onto the glass by the heated foil.

Applying Patina

Patinas change the silver color of soldered seams (and leaded joints) to various shades of either copper or black. Whether or not to apply a patina to your project is entirely up to you. You may enjoy the silvery look of the solder itself.

26. Set the cleaned project on several layers of newspapers. Put on your safety glasses and a pair of rubber gloves. Dip a small piece of cotton rag into the patina and rub the rag along the seams. The less patina you get on the glass, the better. Remoisten the rag as necessary.

As you rub, the solder will begin to change color. As soon as the seams are the desired shade, turn the panel over and repeat to coat the seams on the other side. Don't forget to apply patina to the soldered border.

27. The minute you're finished, clean the entire project again, this time with liquid dishwashing detergent and water; the patina must not be allowed to sit on the glass.

28. Rinse the project well and dry thoroughly with clean rags. Congratulations—you're finished!

ROBERTA KATZ-MESSENGER

Chapter Eight: Working with Lead Came

Leading—the process of assembling glass panels with lead came—is in some ways easier than copper foiling. Because the cut edges of the glass are hidden under the flanges of the came, perfectly smooth edges on your glass aren't quite as important. Leading does present its own challenges, however. In this chapter, you'll learn how to deal with them—and enjoy them—as you assemble your first leaded panel.

Tools and Materials

Basic tool set

Enlarged copy of Figure 2 (on page 48)

Cut glass pieces (see Chapter 6)

Dishwashing detergent

Rags

36" (91.4 cm) of U-shaped zinc came

H-shaped lead came

Horseshoe nails

50/50 solder

Flux and flux brushes

2 lath strips, each at least 12" (30.5 cm) long

3/4" (1.9 cm) brads

1/16" (1.6 mm) brazing rod or heavy-gauge pretinned copper
    wire

Needlenose pliers

Wire cutters

Gray glazing compound mixture

Clear, adhesive-backed plastic (see Step 19)

Newspapers

Gloves

Dust mask

Scrub brushes

Whiting, patching plaster, or plaster of paris

What to Do

Borders

U-shaped zinc, lead, or brass came or H-shaped lead came
can all serve as borders for leaded panels. For square or rectangular panels, we suggest zinc came; it's strong, lighter than
lead, and provides excellent support.

1. Because this project is bordered in zinc came, you must
add a perimeter line to your pattern. To do this, tighten the
zinc into a bench vise or stabilize it on your work surface by
hammering a couple of horseshoe nails on either side of it.
Then, using a hacksaw, cut off a small scrap. Use this scrap
and the instructions on pages 46-47 to create the perimeter
line on your pattern.

2. Take a look at Photo 1. Place the pattern on your work
board or bench and construct a lath jig on top of it, as
described in Step 10 on pages 52-53, but be sure that the
inner edges of the two lath strips are aligned with the perimeter line rather than with the cut line.

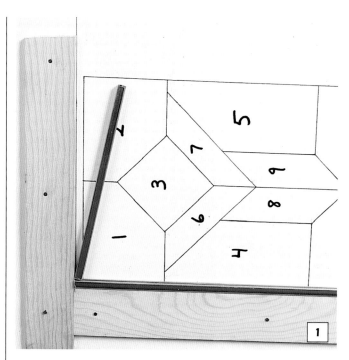

3. Cut two 10-5/8" (27 cm) and two 5-7/8" (14.9 cm) pieces
of zinc came. Note that whenever you cut came, be it lead,
zinc, or brass, you should check to see that the flanges
haven't been pinched out of alignment by the lead loppers or
saw. If they have, run your lathekin through the channel to
widen it again. Also check zinc and brass came for straight-
ness by placing the came flat on your work surface. If the
came doesn't touch the surface along its entire length, use
your hands and/or lathekin to straighten it.

Position one long and one short piece of zinc as shown in
Photo 1, making sure that the left-hand end of the longer
piece meets the vertical lath strip. The position of this longer
came will prove important when you create hooks for your
finished project. To hold each piece of came in position, hammer a couple of horseshoe nails along its length and one at
its free end.

Leading Up

Leading up a panel is the process of assembling a panel by
shaping and cutting lead came to fit between each piece of
glass, and then assembling the glass and leading.

4. Stretch a length of lead came (see "Lead Vise" on page 27).

5. Slip glass piece #1 into the right angle formed by the
pieces of border came. Check to see that the visible edges of
the glass align with the interior cut lines on the pattern.

6. Hold a short length of lead onto the upper edge of piece #1, with one end against the border came to the left. Using the point of a horseshoe nail, mark the lead a short distance from the point at which the pattern line meets the pattern lines for piece #3. The lead shouldn't extend all the way to the end of this line, as room must be left for the flanges of the came that will meet the came you're sizing.

7. Using your lead loppers (or lead knife), cut the came at the mark.

8. Fit the cut lead over the top edge of piece #1. If necessary, hold it in place by hammering a horseshoe nail next to it. Cut the other two pieces of lead to fit around piece #1 in a similar fashion, being careful to allow room for the flanges of abutting pieces of came.

9. Insert glass piece #2 next, checking it against its pattern lines. The glass in your panel should have a little play, so aim for a relaxed fit.

10. Read "Tech Tips: The Zen of Leading" on pages 62-63 before continuing. Then study Photo 2. Assemble the entire panel by fitting the pieces of glass, checking them against the pattern lines, and cutting pieces of lead to fit around them. Note that the lead which will meet the zinc border came along the upper side of the panel has been cut short enough to allow the border came to be fitted over the edge of the glass.

11. When all the glass pieces are in place, slip the last two zinc border pieces in place, holding them in position with horseshoe nails. Use your tape measure to check the dimensions of the finished panel and a right angle to check the four corners for square, adjusting the zinc as necessary (see Photo 3).

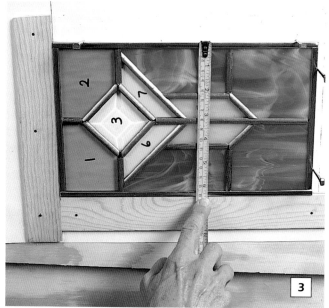

12. Check for gaps between pieces of lead or between the lead and zinc border. If you see any, cut a scrap of lead came through the center of the heart, shape it to fill the gap, and drop it in place (see Photo 4).

Soldering Joints

After the panel has been assembled, the lead joints must be soldered together. Review the information on soldering provided in Chapter Seven. Be sure that your work area has adequate ventilation.

Soldering lead joints differs somewhat from soldering copper foil seams, and artists vary widely in their preferred techniques. We'll offer two methods here; take your pick—or try them both!

Method 1: Touch the solder wire to the joint between the leads and bring the tip down onto the solder, pressing it onto the joint to melt about 1/4" (6 mm) of solder. Lift the iron straight up as soon as the solder has melted.

Method 2: At the junction of the cames, apply solder to about 1/4" of one piece of came and then to 1/4" of the other (or others). Then blend these separate solder applications by smoothing the solder where they meet (see Photos 5, 6, and 7).

5

TECH TIP

T H E   Z E N   O F   L E A D I N G

—Ideally, your cut glass should match the lines on your pattern exactly, with just enough room between each piece to accommodate the heart of the lead came. You will find, however, that leading up a panel is a mysterious (dare we say magical?) process, not an exact science.

You'll discover that parallel pieces such as borders and grids tend to shrink as you lead them up. Remember the tolerance that your pattern shears created and assemble these pieces without compressing them. You'll be amazed at how solder and glazing tighten up a panel that seems loose.

Conversely, curvilinear designs tend to grow. If your panel continues to grow out of shape as you assemble it, back up. Are all the cames short enough to allow abutting cames to seat completely? Do all curved cames match the shape of the glass around which they wrap? Are all pieces of glass (especially heavily textured pieces) completely seated in their cames? Adjust the leading as necessary.

If a piece of glass still doesn't seem to fit, remove the came from it so you can see the relationship between the edges of the pieces of glass. You may need to groze or grind.

Finally, as you reach the outer two borders of your panel, you may size the border glass pieces slightly larger or smaller to ensure that the outer dimensions of the completed panel are correct.

—When assembling large panels, tapping a piece of glass may help to ensure a good fit in the came. Place a small block of wood against the glass edge and tap the wood gently with a hammer. A clothespin with one leg sawed off makes an excellent alternative to a block of wood; just place the sawed-off corner against the edge of the glass, and tap the rounded head of the clothespin.

—When leading up large panels, you must hold previously assembled pieces of glass and came in place as you insert others. To do this, hammer horseshoe nails with their flat edges against the came on assembled pieces of glass. To

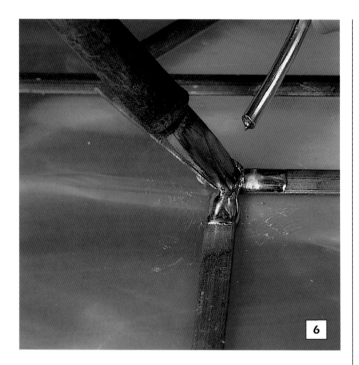

secure glass that's been placed in the panel but hasn't been leaded yet, cut a small scrap of lead, fit it over the outermost edge of the glass, and hammer a horseshoe nail next to the lead scrap. You needn't brace every piece during panel assembly; a few scraps of lead and horseshoe nails here and there will secure the partly assembled panel.

—Ideally, adjoining pieces of lead should be cut to meet each other; large gaps between them will make soldering these joints more difficult, and lead pieces that are too long will throw other pieces of lead out of alignment. Until you've had some practice, cut the came short rather than long. You can always insert patches (see Step 12).

—Sometimes, you'll need to mark and cut the lead at an angle other than 90°. Cut these angles on one flange at a time. To cut extremely sharp angles, remove a short section of the heart of the lead before cutting each flange to the desired angle.

—Occasionally, you'll find that the lead channels aren't wide enough to accommodate the glass. To expand pinched channels, use a lathekin, as shown on page 28.

—When a piece of glass wants to drop below the lead channel rather than fit into it, use the extension on your lathekin or the blade of a knife to lift the glass from underneath while you press it into the channel.

—This project contains only straight-edged pieces of glass. When you're fitting lead to curved pieces, hold the glass in one hand and shape the lead around it. Then mark the lead a little longer than necessary. (Never try to bend lead around corners or sharp points. Use two pieces of lead instead.) Remove the lead from the glass, cut it, replace it on the glass edge, and use the extra length you've allowed to bend the end to the exact shape of the glass. Mark the exact cutting point, remove the lead, and then cut and replace it.

—When leading a rounded or shaped piece of glass, position the lead joint on this piece to meet the joint on another piece, so that both joints may be soldered together simultaneously.

—In designs that incorporate grids and long, straight lead lines, always check before soldering to see that these lines run straight and true. The eye often aims right for these lines in a finished panel, and errors will be noticeable.

Two more tips: When joints in a panel are very close to each other, melt solder over the lead between them to emphasize the design's linear continuity. And when soldering lead to the zinc border, aim for a small, fan-shaped solder joint; solder is difficult to control on zinc. Apply flux to both the zinc and lead and preheat the zinc slightly before soldering. For perfectly shaped border joints, tape the zinc off before fluxing.

13. To remove oxidation, you must scrub the joints with a wire brush immediately before soldering, so we recommend soldering only one joint at a time. Working from the top left-hand corner of the panel, scrub a joint (including the zinc border came where it meets the leading), flux the joint, and apply solder. Continue until all joints have been soldered.

14. Remove the horseshoe nails, turn the panel over (see "Tech Tip: Turning a Panel"), and scrub, flux, and solder the other side. Remove any stray bits of solder from the glass.

Making and Attaching Hooks

Most panels under 2' X 3' (61.0 x 91.4 cm) may be suspended by means of hooks. (Larger panels should always be installed or framed and may also require additional steel supports.) The hook you'll learn how to make here is ideal for panels bordered in zinc. For information on another type of hook, turn to page 57.

15. Insert a length of 1/16"-diameter (1.5 mm) brazing rod or pretinned copper wire all the way through the hollow core of each vertical border came; it should protrude at both ends.

Bend the rod at the bottom to make it parallel to the horizontal border came (see Photo 8).

16. Pull the rod up from the top of the panel so the bent end rests against the bottom of the short border came. Solder the bent portion to the came (see Photo 9).

17. Use needlenose pliers to shape the upper end of the rod into a hook (see Photo 10). Clip off any excess with an old pair of lead loppers or wire cutters.

T U R N I N G   A   P A N E L

Never turn a panel over by gripping it halfway down its sides and lifting it. Stained glass panels aren't rigid; large panels may very well bend or break when lifted in this fashion. Slide the panel to the edge of the bench or work board until it overhangs by almost half its width. Support the bottom edge by cupping it in one hand while you tilt the panel forward with the other; the bench edge and your cupped hand should share the panel's weight. Next, lift the panel to rest vertically on the bench. Then support its front with one hand as you lower it toward you to rest flat again.

If the panel is too large to handle this way, get help! With that help, tilt the panel on the bench, as described in the previous paragraph. Then lower it to the floor, turn it around, lift it vertically up to the bench, and lower it onto the bench until it sets flat again.

You may also turn the panel on the work board. Lift the back edge of the board forward to a vertical position, supporting the panel against it as you do. Holding the panel by its top edge, move the board to the front of the panel. Then bring the board to a flat position by tilting it and the panel forward while sliding the bottom edge of the board back until the board rests flat again.

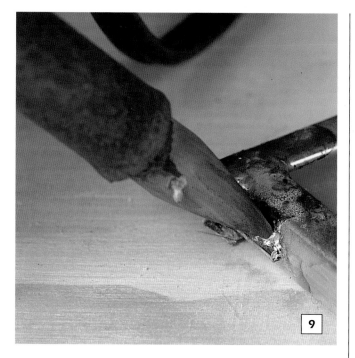

18. To solder each hook to the border, lay the panel flat, use pliers to grip the brazing rod to the edge of the border came, and solder as shown in Photo 11. Hold the hook still; if it moves before the solder has set up, it won't be attached firmly. Turn the panel over to solder the other side of each hook. Then fill the holes at each end of the vertical cames by bracing the panel in a vertical position and applying solder (see Photo 12).

Glazing

To strengthen, waterproof, and insulate the panel, to prevent rattling of the glass, and to darken the cames, your panel must be glazed.

19. Mix a small amount of mineral spirits with some gray glazing compound. About 3/4 cup of compound will be more than enough for a panel this size, but if you plan to make other leaded glass projects, mix up a larger quantity and store it in a sealed container. (See "Glazing Compound" on page 20-21 for additional information.) If you've used any heavily textured glass in your panel, you may want to cover its surfaces with clear, adhesive-backed plastic, or the glazing compound will embed itself in the glass ridges and will be difficult to remove.

20. Spread newspapers out on your work surface. Put on gloves and a dust mask—and continue to wear them throughout the remaining steps—except, of course, when your panel is at one of the resting stages. Place the panel on the newspapers and spoon out a few tablespoons of mixed glazing compound onto the glass (see Photo 13).

21. Using a circular motion and a scrub brush, work the glazing compound under each flange of lead and under the zinc border (see Photo 14). When you've forced glazing under all the flanges, pick up the excess compound with your brush. (Don't worry about every bit; just remove large globs and smears.)

Cleaning and Finishing

After the panel has been glazed, you must clean away all excess glazing compound and all traces of flux. You may also want to apply a patina.

22. Sprinkle a liberal amount of patching plaster, whiting, or plaster of paris over the panel and rub it gently over the glass as shown in Photo 15. The fine powder will begin to absorb the flux and moisture from the compound.

23. Turn the panel over and repeat on the opposite side. (Note that large panels should be glazed one side at a time.) You'll need to allow the glazing compound a little time to set up before brushing the panel (see the next step). How long this will take will depend on the consistency of the glazing mixture. Test a small area after 15 minutes by starting Step 24. If the compound hasn't set up sufficiently, your brush won't pick it up. Don't wait too long, however! The compound will be very difficult to remove once it has cured.

24. To clean the glazing compound and flux from the glass, use a scrub brush to rub the patching plaster vigorously across the glass; run the brush parallel to each piece of leading. Add more patching plaster if necessary and be sure to use a dry brush that hasn't been used to apply glazing compound.

25. After brushing both sides of the panel, use a skewer, popsicle stick cut at an angle, or sharpened dowel to clean any remaining glazing compound from around the edges of the lead (see Photo 16), being careful not to dig the tool under the flanges. Then dust the panel lightly with plaster again and brush a final time. Your panel should be clean of flux and glazing at this time.

26. If you notice oxidation on the leading, rub it off with fine-grade steel wool or with a steel brush. To darken the lead and polish the solder joints, rub them vigorously with a clean rag. Allow the panel to rest in a flat position for at least 24 hours.

27. If you'd like to apply patina to the soldered joints, you may do so any time after the glazing compound has been allowed to dry for 24 hours. Rub it onto the joints with a rag until the solder has darkened. Then wash the entire panel thoroughly in soapy water and allow it to dry.

28. As a final (optional) step, apply either a high-quality car wax or stained glass finishing compound; either will help prevent the lead from oxidizing and make the glass easy to dust. Rub the wax or compound over the entire panel with a clean rag, allow it to dry, and then buff it off. Be sure to wear a dust mask whenever you buff or brush lead.

29. Pat yourself on the back. Display the panel in a window and enjoy!

16

Chapter Nine: Minor Repairs by Steve Brewer

Let's suppose that the hyperactive six-year-old daughter of visiting friends, who's been left alone for not more than three minutes, has managed to take a baseball bat to your favorite stained glass panel. That glorious piece of hand-blown antique glass right in the center looks like—well—like it's just been whacked with a baseball bat.

While major repairs aren't for beginners, don't despair—many minor repairs are well within their reach. In this section, we'll discuss some repairs you can safely tackle.

Copper Foil Repairs

First, if the soldered seams are relatively intact, make a rubbing of them now to serve as a template pattern.

Unless the glass is already in shards, use an old, disposable cutter to score it in a cross-hatch pattern. Tap the scored glass with the ball on the end of your cutter, and use pliers to break and pull out all but the smallest of shards.

Next, you'll need to remove the copper foil that surrounded the broken glass while leaving the foil on surrounding pieces as intact as possible. Flux the solder bead, reheat the solder, and flick away excess solder with the iron tip. Repeat on the other side of the panel until the foil is barely tinned.

To remove the foil that surrounded the broken glass, heat the thin layer of solder on it, simultaneously pulling the foil away with needlenose pliers. If you end up stripping the foil from sections of undamaged glass, too, don't worry. We'll provide you with the remedy in a moment.

Use your rubbing of the solder seams to make a template, or position the panel over a piece of craft paper and trace the shape of the hole onto it, holding your pencil upright as you do. The distance between the pencil point and the edges of the surrounding glass will approximate the tolerance necessary for the new foil. Cut the template out with scissors, use it to cut a new piece of glass, and foil the new glass.

If you've stripped any of the old copper foil from the surrounding glass, replace as much of it as possible. Then insert the new glass, placing a thin sheet of cardboard under it to keep it level with the surrounding glass. Now for that remedy. To deal with glass that lacks foil, you'll bend a length of stretched, pretinned, 20-gauge copper wire to the same shape as the edge of the old glass and solder it in place as shown in Photo 1. (To stretch the wire, attach one end to any stable object and pull on the other end with pliers.)

First flux and tack-solder one end of the wire in place. Gradually bend it to the shape of the glass edge, tacking it as you go. Each bit of tacking solder should bridge the wire and the foil on the new glass. (To make sharply curved bends, hold any rounded object—a skewer works well—vertically next to the wire, and pull the wire around it.)

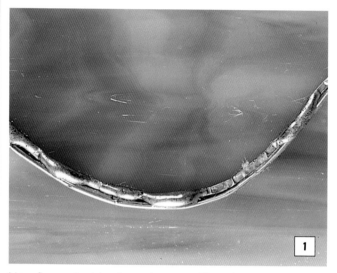

Now flux and solder the entire seam. The wire will act as if it were foil, enabling the solder to form a "came" of sorts to hold both the new glass and old glass together. Repeat on the other side of the panel.

Leaded Glass Repairs

Leaded-glass repair work can be difficult and sometimes involves adding to the existing damage. Think hard before you tackle these jobs!

It's sometimes possible to remove a broken piece by first using lead loppers to cut away rigid soldered sections and then using flat-jawed pliers to lift the flanges surrounding the broken glass (see Photo 2 on the next page). This will only work with lead that is flat in profile, however; rounded came can't be bent upward.

After removing the glass, scrape out the glazing compound from the empty came and cut a new, slightly large piece of glass (see the previous section for details on making templates). Reduce the cut piece to size by grozing or grinding as necessary.

lead flanges, you can create a bridge for new solder in that corner. The solder will attach to the wire and to the heart of the old came to form a perfectly square soldered corner.

As you'll see in Photo 4, it's sometimes necessary to strip away an entire lead flange. If you tack two strips of wire in place as

Place the new glass in the hole, press the lead flanges down again, and burnish them flat with a smooth dowel or rounded piece of hardwood.

Pretinned copper wire makes an excellent bridge over holes in lead came. Take a look at Photo 3. The damaged lead and solder joint have been clipped back at a corner. By bending a short length of wire to 90° and tacking it to the remaining

shown, the solder will flow from one wire to the other, bonding to the remaining heart between them.

Applying black patina to solder that serves as a substitute for lead will improve the appearance of the repaired panel.

On occasion, you may want to preserve a cracked piece of glass that would be difficult to match. Rather than removing the glass, disguise it with an overlay of soldered foil, lead, or wire. Instructions for creating overlays are provided on pages 73 and 74.

Chapter Ten: The Projects

To make any of the projects in this chapter, you'll need a few basic tools and supplies; these are described in Chapters 3 and 4 and listed on page 72.

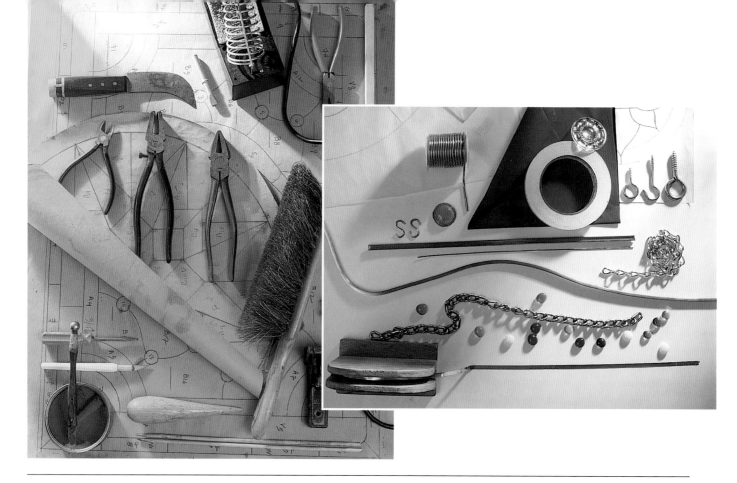

For All Projects

Soldering iron, stand, sponge, and sponge holder

Glass cutter, rag, container, and either kerosene or sewing-machine oil

Bench brush

Lathekin

Pattern shears

Breaking pliers

Running pliers

Slip-joint pliers

Work board or bench

Safety glasses

Hammer

Scissors

Straightedge

Compass

Tape measure

Right angle

Hacksaw

Copper wire (tinned or plain)

Solder

Flux and flux brush

Patching plaster, whiting, or plaster of paris

Scrub brushes

Lattice strips and 3/4" (1.9 cm) brads

Horseshoe nails

Craft, carbon, and tracing paper

Glue stick and spray adhesive

Duct tape or masking tape

Waterproof marker and paint pen

Rubber or latex gloves

Steel wool

Rags

Glass cleaner and paper towels

Newspaper

Finishing compound

Unless otherwise specified, 1/4" (6 mm) zinc border came for straight-sided panels

Glass grinder

For Leaded Glass Projects

Lead loppers or lead knife

Wire brushes

Lead came

Lead vise

Lathekin

Glazing compound

Wooden scrapers

For Copper Foil Projects

Copper foil

Craft knife

Burnishers

Several projects require a few special tools or materials; you'll find these listed with the project instructions. Be sure to check these specific lists before you begin.

Project Tips

Although you'll find it useful to browse through these tips now, you needn't study them carefully. The instructions that accompany the projects will refer you to the specific tips you need to know.

Tracing Bevels and Jewels

Commercial bevels and jewels are not always cut to exact sizes. Whenever you use them in a project, trace their actual shapes onto the pattern before you cut any glass, and cut along the traced lines when you make your templates.

Leading Round Jewels

To wrap round jewels in lead came, find or purchase a rounded object, such as a dowel, that is roughly the same diameter as the jewel. Bend the lead around the dowel in spiral fashion, making as many turns as you have jewels of that size to wrap. Slip the spiraled lead off the dowel and cut it to separate the rounds of lead. Then wrap the leads around the jewels, adjusting lead lengths as necessary.

Bending Short Lengths of Lead

Trying to bend very short lengths of lead by hand is an exercise in futility; you'll find there's not enough lead to grasp. To avoid this problem, use a pair of pliers to bend the lead before cutting it to the necessary length.

Balancing Solder Lines

If you wrap the exterior edges of a foiled project with the same width of foil as you use on the interior seams, the interior seams will appear wider than the cold-soldered border, as the solder on the former covers two widths of foil. To balance the solder lines, wrap the exterior edges with a slightly wider foil. Use a craft knife to trim the margins where the wider foil overlaps the narrower.

Reinforcement for Copper Foil Panels

One way to reinforce copper foil panels is to insert copper restrip between the foiled edges of the glass or against the exterior edges of border pieces. Restrip is fairly easy to bend. On exterior borders, hold it in place with horseshoe nails until it is tacked in place and form the cold-soldered bead right over it.

Short lengths of fine-gauge copper wire placed on top of interior seams or along the outer edges of foiled border glass will also reinforce soldered seams. Forming a solder bead over the wire will disguise it completely.

Preventing Split Foil

Copper foil tends to split when it's wrapped around interior curves. When foiling moderate inside curves, first press the foil—and do use a narrow one—to the edge of the glass. Then use a wooden skewer to stretch the foil gradually over one surface of the glass by slowly tilting the skewer ever closer to that surface. Repeat to press the other margin in place.

To foil sharp interior curves, first press a small piece of foil over the sharpest portion of the curve (where a split would be most likely to occur); wrap this foil "saddle" across rather than along the glass edge. Then apply the perimeter foil in the usual manner, covering the saddle as you do. If the perimeter foil splits at the curve, the saddle will still provide a base for the solder. Trim the exposed ends of the saddle with a craft knife.

Copper Foil Overlays

Trace the pattern of the overlay onto a piece of tracing paper. (It's a good idea to add an extra "tab" to the edges that will touch a seam or border; this tab may be folded over the edge of the glass to help prevent the overlay from lifting when the foil is heated.) Tape the tracing paper on top of a sheet of copper foil. To impress the traced outline onto the foil, retrace it, firmly, with a ballpoint pen. Separate the sheets and use scissors to cut out the foil.

After cutting, foiling, and temporarily assembling the glass pieces, remove the backing from the overlays, position them on the glass, and burnish them securely. (Don't forget to burnish the tabs in place, too.) The glass must be absolutely clean for the overlays to adhere properly. Flux and solder all seams, and then flux and apply solder to cover the overlays. One warning: Applying a great deal of heat to the glass will crack it, so either work quickly or allow the glass to cool off between solder applications.

Burnishing Foiled Nuggets

Burnishing foiled nuggets one by one is a task for the truly insane; don't try it! Roughen the nugget edges on a grinder. Clean, dry , and wrap each nugget in foil, pressing the foil in place with your fingers. Place the foiled nuggets in a plastic container, snap on the lid, and shake the container briskly. As they rub elbows, the nuggets will burnish each other.

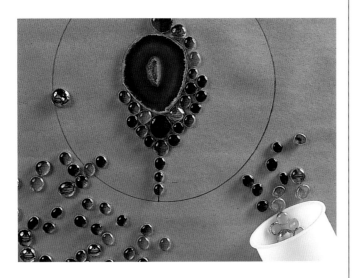

Positioning and Soldering Grouped Nuggets

Grouped nuggets make an attractive addition to many panels. Before you cut any glass in a panel with a nugget grouping, foil and burnish the nuggets and arrange them on the pattern, leaving a bit of space between each one. To establish the cut lines for the glass that surrounds them, trace around their exterior borders onto the pattern. After the panel has been tacked together, fill the spaces between the nuggets with solder.

Creating Illusions with Lead

Cutting an interior right angle in glass just isn't possible. What is possible is to cut your lead came in such a way that the viewer thinks you've achieved this miraculous feat! For an example of this leading trick, study the corners of the project on page 77.

Take a good look at Figure 1. As you can see, what appears to be a 90° interior cut in the glass is in fact a curved cut. The vertical strip of came has been cut as usual. The horizontal strip, however, has had some of its heart removed. Its flanges, which meet the adjoining came at a right angle, disguise the curves in the glass beneath.

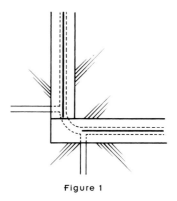

Figure 1

Smooth Solder Beads on Heavily Textured Glass

Copper foil wrapped around heavily textured glass will dip up and down with the glass and will create an uneven solder bead unless you use this tip. First tack the foiled pieces of glass together. Then, as you solder the bead, hold a fluxed piece of fine-gauge copper wire directly over the outer edge of the uneven foil (see the photo on the opposite page). The solder will adhere to the wire to create a smooth bead.

Incorporating Objects That Aren't Glass

Many attractive objects, including geodes, seashells, and semi-precious stones, can be added to your copper foil projects as highlights. Just wrap their edges with foil and solder them in among pieces of glass. Geodes, by the way, are quite easy to score and break .

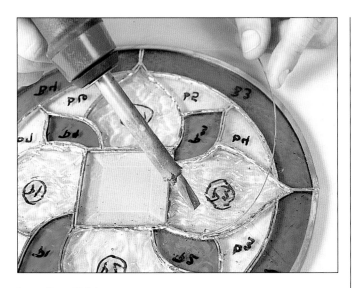

Leading Grids

In leaded panels that incorporate grids, weave the leading (see Figure 2), rather than leading up with long strips of came. Using shorter lengths and placing them in an irregular pattern will strengthen the panel considerably and will make it easier to keep the lead lines straight.

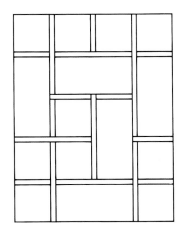

Figure 2

Protecting Mirrors from Flux and Patina

To protect mirror backing from corrosive flux and patina, cut the mirror to shape, and apply two coats of clear lacquer to every cut edge and to the back itself, allowing time between each coat for thorough drying.

Making and Attaching Hinges

Hinges are available through stained-glass suppliers, but they're very easy to make from 1/16" (1.5 mm) brass brazing rod and hollow brass tubing with an I.D. (interior diameter) large enough to accommodate the brazing rod. Measure the edge of the lid you wish to hinge, and cut a piece of hollow brass tubing just a bit shorter than that edge. Solder the tubing to the foiled edge of the lid. Then cut two short pieces of brazing rod, bending each one to a 90° angle (see Figure 3). Insert one end of each brazing rod into one end of the tube, and solder the portion that extends from the tube into the seam on the frame of the box (see Figure 4). Be careful not to get any solder into the tubing!

Buy the brazing rod at a welding-supply store and the hollow brass tubing at a hobby shop.

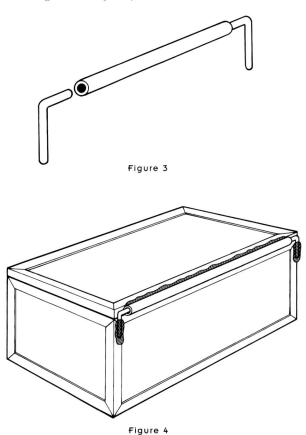

Figure 3

Figure 4

Lamp Assembly

First, assemble each flat panel separately by foiling and soldering together the component parts. Cold-solder the top and bottom edges of each one. (If you're going to delay assembly at all, be sure to tin all foil to protect it from corrosion.) When foiling panels, you may want to use a wider foil on exterior borders.

Next, to shape the lamp shade, tack the panels together, one by one, at their adjoining seams. As you do this, position the panels so that the inner corners of adjoining seams are aligned. Work on a carpet remnant or on a single layer of towel so the panels won't slip as you work. When all the panels have been tacked together, check to see that the shade is shaped correctly. If you need to make adjustments, remelt the tacking solder and re-tack as necessary. Be patient! This process may take a bit of time. View the shade from the top; doing so will give you a clear view of any misalignments. When you're through tacking, install the spider or vent cap (see "Making and Attaching Spiders" below).

If the shade is relatively small, turn it over and solder the beads on the inside seams first. For larger shades or for any shade that feels unstable, first fill the exterior seams with enough solder to hold the panels together securely. If you don't take this extra step, the foil on large lamps may tear away from the panels when you turn the lamp upside down to reach its interior seams. As you solder each seam, you'll need to prop the lamp in such a way that the seams are parallel to the ground or you'll find that it's almost impossible to shape even solder beads.

After the interior has been soldered, solder the exterior seams, and touch up any edge soldering as needed.

Stained glass shades must have adequate ventilation in order to allow the heat of the bulb to escape. Never use vent caps that lack ventilation holes. Purchase ceramic sockets whenever possible as the metallic ones include components that may melt or char.

Making and Attaching Spiders

A spider, which is attached to the opening at the top of a glass lamp shade, serves three purposes: It provides strength to the lamp panel, allows the shade to be attached to a base, and allows the heat of the bulb to escape.

To make a spider, you'll need a brass washer with a 3/8" (1 cm) hole in it and several pieces of 1/16" (1.5 mm) or 3/32" (.75 mm) brass brazing rod. Decide how many legs the spider must have, keeping in mind that the legs will be soldered into the seams between the panels of the shade. Divide 360° by the number of legs to calculate the angles between each pair of legs (see Figure 5).

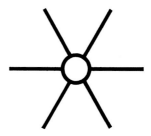

Figure 5

Cut the brazing rod into pieces long enough to extend from the hole in the washer to about 1" (2.5 cm) beyond the seams between panels. (The extra length will be bent and soldered into the seam.) Flux one surface of the washer and tin it. Flux the end of each leg and tack the legs to the washer. Position the tacked assembly on the top of the lamp and check to see that each leg is positioned over a seam. Adjust their positions as needed by remelting the tacking solder.

Next, apply more solder to the washer, until the spaces between the legs have been completely filled and the solder is as thick as the legs. (For extra strength in hanging lamps, solder another washer on top of the legs, aligning the holes in the washers carefully.)

Spiders should be attached to the shade after the panels have been tacked together. Place the spider, soldered side down, on top of the shade and bend each leg down into a tacked exterior seam. (For multi-panel and hanging lamps, bend the spider legs to fit along the interior seams.) Then complete soldering the beads on the shade, burying the legs in the solder beads as you do.

■ COMPASS-POINT MANDALA

Take a close look at one of the square glass corners of this panel. See anything strange? You're right: There appears to be an impossible right-angled cut in the clear glass adjoining each one. Don't worry! We're not asking the impossible of you. What you see is an illusion created with lead came.

SUGGESTED SIZE: 17-1/4" X 17-1/4" (43.8 X 43.8 cm)

■ SPECIAL TOOLS AND MATERIALS

- Sheet metal for button-shaped overlays (optional)

■ TECH TIPS

To give this panel greater visual interest, the artist has used different widths of lead. Feel free to do the same.

See "Creating Illusions with Lead" on page 74.

If you look closely, you'll see four button-shaped overlays on the leading at the four points of the compass. Cut the buttons from sheet metal and then flux and tin them. Place a button on top of a soldered joint and use your soldering iron to heat the button's upper surface. As the solder on the joint underneath begins to melt, the tinned button will adhere to it.

■ HOOK INSTRUCTIONS

See Steps 15-18 on pages 64-65.

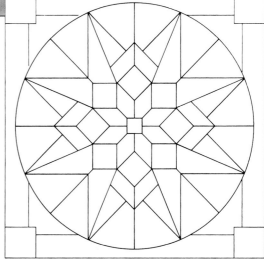

■ VERTICAL WINDOW PANEL

This leaded pattern, designed for a beginners' class, will test your new cutting skills without posing challenges you can't possibly meet, so relax! Focus your energy on selecting glass that pleases you and on making good use of the textures and streaks of color in it.

■ TECH TIPS

Take a look at the cut lines marked A and B. These are literally impossible to make; interior 90° cuts just won't work. See "Creating Illusions with Lead" on page 74 to find out how this look is achieved.

Note that the artist has added visual interest to this panel by using a different lead width on the inner edge of the border.

■ HOOK INSTRUCTIONS

See Steps 15-18 on pages 64-65.

SUGGESTED SIZE: 16-1/4" X 28" (41.2 X 71.1 CM)

■ BUTTERFLIES

By selecting a semi-antique for her background, the artist has managed to make these colorful butterflies, with their mottled glass wings, look as if they're actually flying.

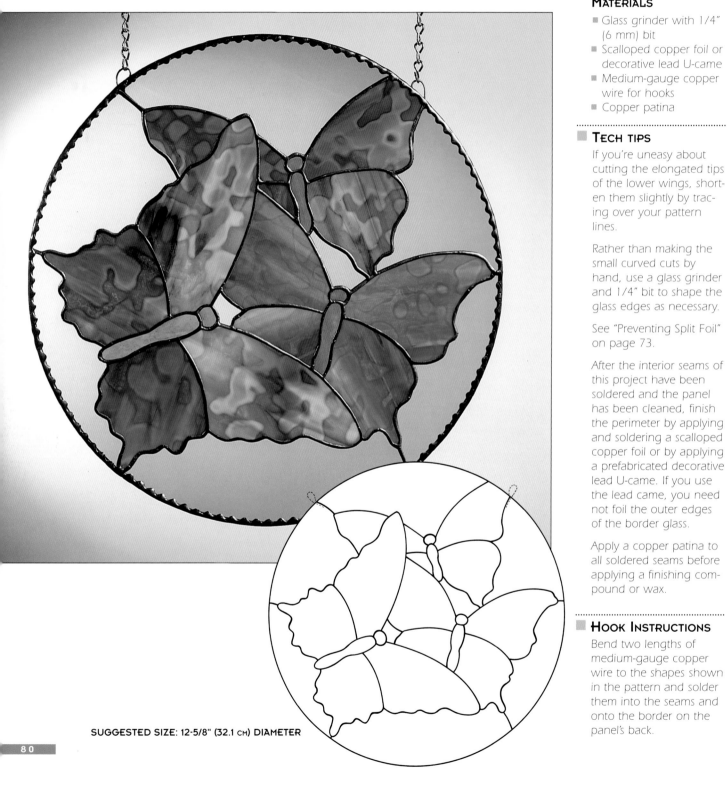

SUGGESTED SIZE: 12-5/8" (32.1 CM) DIAMETER

■ SPECIAL TOOLS AND MATERIALS

- ■ Glass grinder with 1/4" (6 mm) bit
- ■ Scalloped copper foil or decorative lead U-came
- ■ Medium-gauge copper wire for hooks
- ■ Copper patina

■ TECH TIPS

If you're uneasy about cutting the elongated tips of the lower wings, shorten them slightly by tracing over your pattern lines.

Rather than making the small curved cuts by hand, use a glass grinder and 1/4" bit to shape the glass edges as necessary.

See "Preventing Split Foil" on page 73.

After the interior seams of this project have been soldered and the panel has been cleaned, finish the perimeter by applying and soldering a scalloped copper foil or by applying a prefabricated decorative lead U-came. If you use the lead came, you need not foil the outer edges of the border glass.

Apply a copper patina to all soldered seams before applying a finishing compound or wax.

■ HOOK INSTRUCTIONS

Bend two lengths of medium-gauge copper wire to the shapes shown in the pattern and solder them into the seams and onto the border on the panel's back.

■ GEODE SUNSET

The geode sun in this lovely panel is set off exquisitely by the background and foreground glass. Its foiled interior is framed in a leaded border.

■ SPECIAL TOOLS AND MATERIALS

- 1 geode large enough to cut to sun shape (see pattern)
- Lead H-and U-came for border
- Medium-gauge copper wire for hooks

■ TECH TIPS

To create the sense of perspective so important to this design, select glass of greater density for the foreground.

See "Incorporating Objects That Aren't Glass" on page 74.

There's no need to foil the outer edges of the pieces that abut the lead H-came on the border. Remember not to solder the foiled seams all the way to their outer edges, or you won't be able to fit the lead came over them. To hold the border in place as you tack the panel together, hammer a few horseshoe nails around its exterior.

■ HOOK INSTRUCTIONS

Shape two short lengths of copper wire into hooks, bending the legs to stretch along the H-came and right into the nearest solder beads. Solder the hooks to the back of the panel, making sure that they're firmly embedded in the solder beads on the seams, or the weight of the panel will pull the H-came away from the glass.

SUGGESTED SIZE: 12-1/2" (31.8 cm) DIAMETER

■ WHERE ON EARTH?

Bold colors and wonderful textures can transform a simple leaded panel into a breathtaking personal vision. Notice, too, how the artist has complemented the colors in the central piece of glass by surrounding it with various shades of those colors.

■ TECH TIPS

See "Bending Short Lengths of Lead" on page 73.

Unless you plan to have this panel installed, we recommend framing it in 1/4" (6 mm) zinc U-came rather than lead.

■ HOOK INSTRUCTIONS

See Steps 15-18 on pages 64-65.

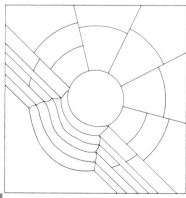

SUGGESTED SIZE: 18" X 18" (45.7 X 45.7 cm)

■ VICTORIAN HEART AND WINGED HEART

Designed to display tear-drop shaped prisms from old chandeliers, these stunning hearts involve no complex cuts. In the Victorian Heart, the artist has accentuated the graceful design lines by cutting a streaky cathedral glass to incorporate the streaks. The Winged Heart is cut entirely from glue chip.

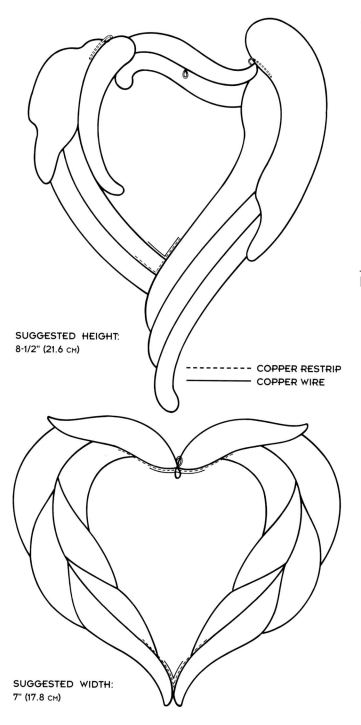

SUGGESTED HEIGHT:
8-1/2" (21.6 CM)

- - - - - - - - - - COPPER RESTRIP
———————— COPPER WIRE

SUGGESTED WIDTH:
7" (17.8 CM)

■ SPECIAL TOOLS AND MATERIALS (FOR EITHER HEART)

- Copper restrip or medium-gauge copper wire
- 3" (7.6 cm) prism (Victorian Heart)
- 1-1/2" or 2" (3.8 or 5.1 cm) prism (Winged Heart)
- Medium-gauge copper wire for hooks
- Fine-gauge copper wire for prisms (optional)
- Copper jack chain

■ TECH TIPS

Look for the prism at a lamp shop or antique store, or order one through a renovator's supply catalogue. If it's missing its original wire, simply use fine-gauge copper wire to attach it to its hook on the heart.

See "Balancing Solder Lines" on page 73.

See "Reinforcement for Copper Foil Panels" on page 73. Locations for either restrip or wire are marked on the patterns.

■ HOOK INSTRUCTIONS

For the Victorian Heart, bend three lengths of medium-gauge copper wire as indicated in the pattern. Solder the two tear-drop shaped hooks into the appropriate seams on the back of the heart. Be sure to solder the third, circular hook for the tear-drop into the interior seam, not onto the border. To suspend this heart, attach a length of jack chain to the wire loops on either side.

For the Winged Heart, bend a length of medium-gauge copper wire into a figure eight and solder it to the heart's back surface as indicated in the pattern. Attach the prism to the lower loop and the copper jack chain to the upper loop.

■ ANGELFISH

A small but truly lovely project, this foiled angelfish makes excellent use of overlays and wire extensions.

SUGGESTED SIZE: (FIN TIP TO FIN TIP) 7-1/2 " (19.1 cm)

■ SPECIAL TOOLS AND MATERIALS

- ■ Sheet of copper foil for overlays
- ■ Medium-gauge copper wire for "feelers"
- ■ Fine-gauge copper wire for hooks

■ TECH TIPS

The shaded portions of the pattern represent overlays. See "Copper Foil Overlays" on pages 73-74.

To create the dot in the fish eye, allow the soldered overlay to cool, reflux the eye, and apply a drop of solder right into its center, heating the overlay solder just enough to make the drop adhere.

Before making the two "feelers," cold-solder the borders of the fish. Then bend two pieces of medium-gauge copper wire to the shapes shown in the pattern. Next, bend about 1/4" (6 mm) of the front end of each wire to conform to the border of the fish's head. Solder these bent portions to the border; also solder each wire where it meets the lower fin.

Apply copper patina to all soldered areas before applying a finishing compound or wax.

■ HOOK INSTRUCTIONS

To make hooks, shape and attach two short pieces of fine-gauge copper wire as shown in the pattern.

HUMMINGBIRD AND TRUMPET VINE

We've photographed this small but unusual copper foil project from the back, to show you how the delicate hummingbird and colorful trumpet vine are attached to the hoop.

SPECIAL TOOLS AND MATERIALS

- 7-3/4" (19.7 cm) brass or brass-plated hoop
- Brass brazing rod for stem
- Fine-gauge copper wire for bird's eye

TECH TIPS

Brass hoops are carried by many craft-supply stores.

Bend the brazing rod to the shape of the stem. Arrange the foiled glass and the stem on the pattern, and position the hoop over the bird's tail as shown. Tack the glass, hoop, and stem together, fluxing the hoop and stem where solder will be applied. Solder the seams on both sides.

To make the beak, fold a short length of copper foil along its length so that the adhesive surface sticks to itself. Then cut the folded foil to shape, position as shown, and solder in place.

To make the eye, bend a short piece of fine-gauge copper wire into a circle, leaving a tail of wire extending from it. Flux the wire and fill the circle with solder. Then position the wire on the bird's head and solder the wire tail to the seam.

Cold-solder all borders and apply copper patina before applying finishing compound or wax.

HOOK INSTRUCTIONS

Use a commercial hook and chain as shown in the photo or, for a more delicate look, tie a piece of monofilament fishing line to the hoop.

SUGGESTED HOOP SIZE: 7-3/4" (19.7 cm)

■ FREE-FORM GEODE PANEL

In case you're wondering why there isn't a pattern provided for this copper foil panel, it's because you'll create the free-form, spontaneous design as you go.

■ SPECIAL TOOLS AND MATERIALS

- Nuggets in colors of your choice
- 1 geode
- Lead U-came for border
- Medium-gauge copper wire for hook arrangement

■ TECH TIPS

See "Positioning and Soldering Grouped Nuggets" on page 74.

To create the pattern, start by drawing a circle of any size. Divide the circle into three parts by bisecting it with one line and adding another line to meet the first. Position the geode to cover the point where the lines intersect and trace its outline onto the pattern. Arrange the nuggets around the geode and trace around the outer edges of the grouping to define the cut lines for your three pieces of art glass.

See "Burnishing Foiled Nuggets" on page 74.

Because this panel is framed in lead U-came, there's no need to foil the outer edges of the exterior pieces of glass.

■ HOOK INSTRUCTIONS

The hook arrangement for this panel consists of a doubled and twisted length of medium-gauge copper wire which, because it is soldered to the lower half of the panel, prevents the weight of the panel from pulling the U-came away from the glass. To twist the wire, insert an eye-hook into an electric drill. Thread the wire through the eyehook and have a friend grip the loose ends securely with a pair of pliers. Turn on the drill and allow the eyehook to turn until the wire has been twisted to the shape shown in the photo (most clearly shown at the hook ends). Twist the free ends of the wire into a secure hook. Then tack the wire to the outer edge of the U-came on the lower half of the panel.

■ CHRIS'S VALIANT ATTEMPT

This panel, one of Marty's designs for beginners, was my first stab at cutting and leading in over 20 years. I was incredibly proud of myself, until I placed the finished piece in a sunny window and noticed the lopsided jewel. Oh well. I gave the panel to someone who loves me too much to complain, and Marty has included a tip here to help you avoid this leading problem.

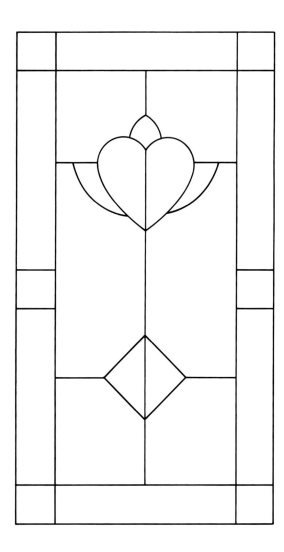

ENLARGE PATTERN 325% FOR 2"- SQUARE (5.1 CM) JEWEL

■ SPECIAL TOOLS AND MATERIALS
- One 2"-square (5.1 cm) jewel (optional)

■ TECH TIPS
See "Tracing Bevels and Jewels" on page 73.

If you prefer, replace the jewel with a cut piece of glass.

When leading the square jewel in this panel, use Figure 1 as a lead-cutting guide.

■ HOOK INSTRUCTIONS
See page 57. Solder the hooks to the top of the zinc border came.

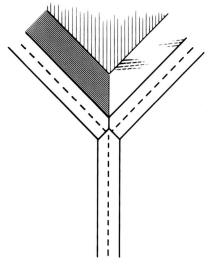

Figure 1

■ VICTORIAN PANEL

This classic Victorian panel proves its artist's sensitivity to the colors and textures of her glass. Although the panel will take some time to cut and assemble, beginners shouldn't hesitate to select it as one of their first projects.

■ SPECIAL TOOLS AND MATERIALS

- 38 jewels, 3/4"-diameter (1.9 cm)

■ TECH TIPS

See "Tracing Bevels and Jewels" on page 73.

See "Burnishing Foiled Nuggets" and "Positioning and Soldering Grouped Nuggets" on page 74.

For a lighter look, the artist has foiled the seven jewels on each side of the panel, as well as the glass around them. If you'd rather lead them up, by all means do so. See "Leading Round Jewels" on page 73. Just be sure to use the appropriate pair of shears when you cut out your templates!

The multiple borders on this piece add strength to the panel, as do the deliberately staggered lead breaks in them.

■ HOOK INSTRUCTIONS

See Steps 15-18 on pages 64-65.

ENLARGE BY 675% TO ACCOMMODATE STANDARD SIZE JEWELS

93

■ PURPLE AND MAUVE MANDALA

Here's a foiled panel framed in lead U-came that should test some of the cutting skills you learned in Chapter 5. If you select colors with as much care as the artist has, you should end up with a panel worthy of hanging in any brightly lit window.

■ SPECIAL TOOLS AND MATERIALS

- One 2"-diameter (5.1 cm) jewel
- Lead U-came for border
- Heavy-gauge copper wire for hooks

■ TECH TIPS

See "Tracing Bevels and Jewels" on page 73.

When you wrap a foiled panel in lead U-came, there's no need to foil the outer edges of the border glass. Just run the foil to the ends of the interior seams. Remember not to run the solder beads all the way to the outer ends of the seams, or you won't be able to wrap the lead around them.

■ HOOK INSTRUCTIONS

Each of the two U-shaped hooks on this panel (see photo) is embedded in both the front and back solder beads and is soldered to the lead border came as well. If the hook ends were attached only to the border, the weight of the panel would pull the lead came away from the glass.

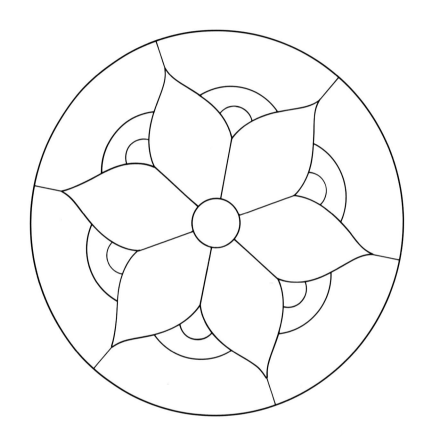

ENLARGE PATTERN BY 400% TO ACCOMMODATE 2"-DIAMETER (5.1 CM) JEWEL

■ REPETITIONS

Want to practice your glass-cutting skills? By the time you've finished this copper foil panel, you should be a top ranked cutter-of-curves!

■ TECH TIPS

Number your templates, and number each piece of glass when the templates are removed. Unless you can identify the pieces in this project, slight cutting variations will drive you crazy when it comes time to assemble the foiled glass on your pattern.

To keep from cracking off the sharp points of the purple pieces, cut them slightly large and make use of your glass grinder to shape the points.

■ HOOK INSTRUCTIONS

This panel has been bordered in zinc, framed in wood, and suspended by means of eyehooks inserted into the wooden frame. Any good cabinet-maker should be able to create a wooden frame for you, but zinc U-came alone will also work. To create hooks for a zinc-framed panel, see Steps 15-18 on pages 64-65.

SUGGESTED SIZE: 15-5/8" X 28-3/4" (39.7 X 73 CM)

■ STUDY IN TEXTURES

Here's a great example of what serious consideration to glass selection can do for your finished panel. The artist has considered three aspects of his glass very carefully indeed: its color, its grain, and above all, its texture.

■ TECH TIPS

In order to accentuate the heavy texture of the border glass, the artist has chosen to create uneven solder seams in this copper foil panel. If he'd wanted to make the edges of the beads smoother, he could have used the information in "Smooth Solder Beads on Heavily Textured Glass" (see page 74).

■ HOOK INSTRUCTIONS

This panel has been framed in wood and is suspended by means of eyehooks inserted into the frame. Any good cabinetmaker should be able to create a wooden frame for you, but you may also use zinc U-came and create hooks as described in Steps 15-18 on pages 64-65.

SUGGESTED SIZE: 12-3/4" X 29-1/2" (32.4 X 75 cm)

■ MAN WITH PIPE

The artist derived this wonderful design from a small silver finial on an Art Deco cigarette box. Three shades of gray glass accentuate its elegant simplicity.

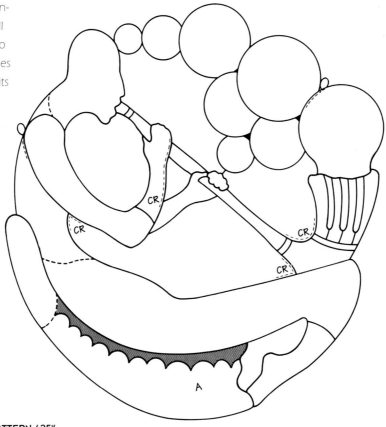

CR – copper restrip

ENLARGE PATTERN 425%.

■ SPECIAL TOOLS AND MATERIALS

- Copper restrip
- Sheet of copper foil for overlay
- Medium-gauge copper wire for hooks
- Copper patina
- Glass grinder with 1/8" (3 mm) bit

■ TECH TIPS

To replicate this piece, you'll need three shades of grey glass: a dark grey for the rock, a medium grey for the man and for sections of the pipe, and a light grey for other sections of the pipe. For the bubbles, select a glass that implies roundness, one with gently contoured streaks, or try a glass with a fragile look, such as a seedy antique or hand-blown reamy. The background pieces involve some challenging cuts; a semi-antique will work well for these, as it breaks dependably.

Before you cut any glass, note that the shaded portion on piece A is a foil overlay; don't try to cut it out! Also note that we've included some optional cut lines (shown as dotted lines at the neck, waist and back of the rock) for those of you who aren't yet confident with your cutting skills!

Rather than trying to score and break out the man's profile and hands, shape them with a 1/8" grinding bit.

See "Preventing Split Foil" on page 73. Use a relatively narrow foil on the borders of this piece.

See "Reinforcement for Copper Foil Panels" on page 73.

See "Copper Foil Overlays" on pages 73-74.

Apply copper patina to all lead lines before applying a finishing compound or wax.

■ HOOK INSTRUCTIONS

Bend medium-gauge copper wire into two teardrop shaped hooks and solder them into the solder beads on the back of the project, as indicated in the pattern.

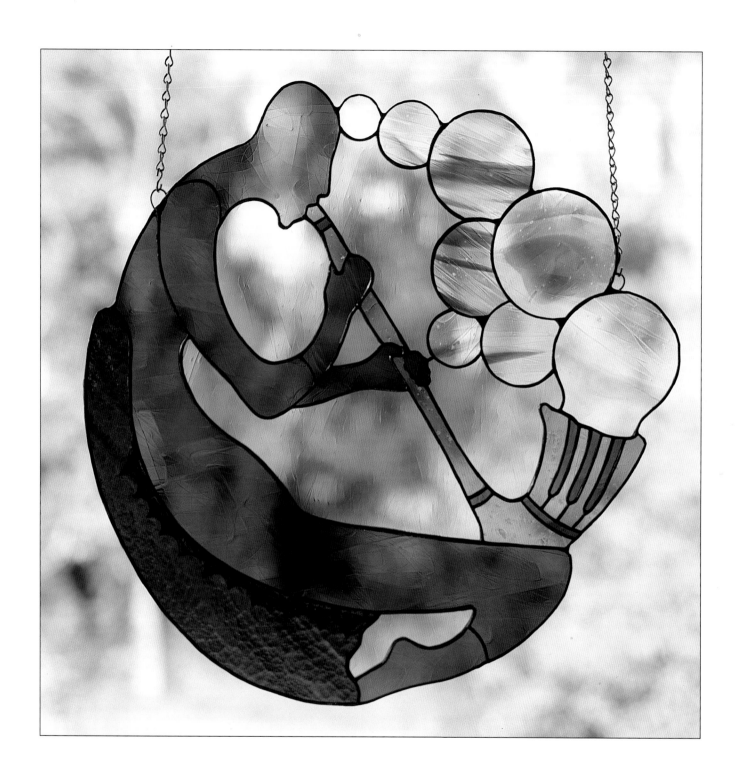

■ BEVELED BOX

This beveled box is a fine example of a project assembled with brass channel. We'll walk you through its construction step by step.

■ SPECIAL TOOLS AND MATERIALS

- 1/8" (3 mm) brass channel
- Wire cutters
- Two 2" x 6" (5.1 x 15.2 cm) bevels
- Two 2" x 3-1/2" (5.1 x 8.9 cm) bevels
- Six 2" x 3" (5.1 x 7.6 cm) bevels
- Brass ornaments, handle, and feet (optional)
- Gold-colored glass marking pen
- See also "Making and Attaching Hinges" on page 75.

■ WHAT TO DO

1. Each of the two 2" x 6" bevels on the back and front of the box is completely wrapped in brass channel. Position a bevel as shown in Figure 1. Mark the channel with a pencil on both its front and back edge and use wire cutters to snip out a 90° notch at each mark. Bend the channel at the notches, overlapping the snipped edges as you do, until the channel wraps around the short edge of the bevel. Mark, cut, and clip the channel at the next two corners, until the bevel is completely wrapped (see Figure 2). Where the two ends of the channel meet, flux and solder to secure.

2. Repeat to wrap the other 6" bevel and the two 3-1/2" side bevels.

3. To assemble the front, back, and sides, stand the front and one side bevel in the corner of the jig as shown in Figure 3. Tack solder the upper edge where they meet. Assemble the other two pieces in the same fashion. Then position the two tacked assemblies to form a rectangle within the jig, and solder all the corners. Repeat on the underside of this assembled frame.

4. To construct the lid, wrap each of the four 2" x 3" bevels in copper foil. Arrange them in a rectangle within the jig and solder the two intersecting seams on both surfaces, leaving a bit of unsoldered foil at the ends of each seam.

5. Solder the brass ornaments to the intersecting seams on the top of the lid, using as little solder as possible. Then wrap the entire four-bevel rectangle in brass channel (see Step 1). On the back of the lid only, solder the channel to the seams by continuing the beads up onto the channel.

6. To make the bottom of the box, place the soldered frame on top of a piece of clear float glass and, using a marker, trace the inner outline of the frame onto the glass. Score, break out, and foil the rectangle.

7. Place the bottom into the box frame and solder it to the brass chan-nel. Turn the frame over and solder the bottom to the outside of the frame as well.

8. Place the lid on the body, aligning it carefully. For information on making and attaching hinges, see page 75. (Commercial hinges are available; feel free to use them instead.)

9. Solder the decorative feet to the bottom of the box and the handle to the front of the lid, using pliers to hold each piece in place as the solder cools. To prevent the lid from falling backward when the box is opened, solder a fine brass or copper chain as shown in the photo.

10. Clean the box thoroughly with dishwashing detergent and water, dry well, and color the soldered areas with the gold marking pen.

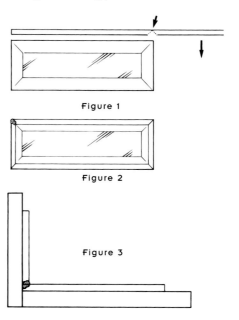

Figure 1

Figure 2

Figure 3

With its optional dividers, this stunning copper foil box will no doubt prove to be a family heirloom, and the night-light shade will be a hit whether you use it in your own home or give it to a lucky friend.

■ SPECIAL TOOLS AND MATERIALS (FOR SHADE)

- One clip for night-light shade (see Figure 1)

Figure 1

■ TECH TIPS (FOR SHADE)

The clip that holds the shade onto the night-light is available through stained glass suppliers. Order one with a miniature bolt, not the snap-on variety.

Cut one A piece and two B pieces (see Figure 2).

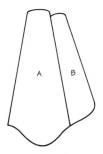

Figure 2

ENLARGE 250%

Foil and tack them together to the shape shown in the photo. Then solder all the seams and borders. Remember that in order to keep the soldered seams smooth, you must keep the seams parallel to the ground as you solder them.

Bend the legs of the clip to the shape of the shade's underside. Then flux and solder them to the interior seams. Also solder the clip to the shade, aiming for as many soldered contact points as possible.

To form the decorative solder drops (see photo), allow the solder beads to cool, reflux, and apply a drop of solder, heating the bead just long enough to make sure that the drop is affixed firmly to it.

■ SPECIAL TOOLS AND MATERIALS (FOR BOX)

- See "Making and Attaching Hinges" on page 75.

■ TECH TIPS (FOR BOX)

Choose glass with color swirls to match the mountains portrayed in the lid (see Pattern D).

Cut two A pieces, one B piece, two C pieces, and the five pieces that make up pattern D. Don't try to score and break out the sharp interior curves on the A pieces. Instead, cut gentler curves and use your glass grinder to shape them to the edges of your templates. Notice that piece D, the lid of the box, is 1/4" (6 mm) wider and longer than the bottom, as it must cover the 1/8"-thick (3 mm) sides of the box frame.

To assemble the box, first foil all the glass except piece B (the bottom of the box), and flux and tin all seams. Then place one A and one C piece upright and upside-down in a jig (see Step 10 on page 52) with the interior corners of their short edges meeting. Tack the adjoining edges together. Tack together the other A and C pieces next, and then tack the two sets together to form a rectangular frame, using the jig to keep the corners square. Run beads along all the outer and inner seams and cold-solder beads along the upper and lower borders.

Check to see that piece B will fit into the frame with just a bit of play; if B is tight, groze or grind its edges. Then foil, flux, and tin it, and solder it into the frame, making sure that it rests above the bottom of the "feet."

To make the optional dividers, measure the interior of the box and cut three pieces of glass to size, as shown in pattern B. Foil and assemble the dividers into a single unit by tacking them together and running beads along all seams except for the bottom edges, which will sit on the floor of the box. Insert the divider assembly and tack its four corners to the seams of the frame.

Foil, flux, and solder the lid panel. To make a hinge and attach the lid to the box, see page 75.

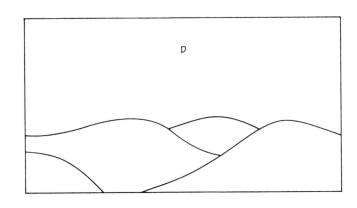

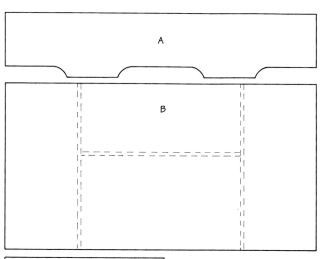

A   1¾" X 10¾" (4.4 X 27.3 cm)
B   5½" X 10¾" (14 X 27.3 cm)
C   1¾" X 5½" (4.4 X 14 cm)
D   5¾" X 11" (14.6 X 27.9 cm)

■ BABY BLOCKS QUILTING PATTERN

The amazing three-dimensional quality of this panel is the result both of its geometric form and of careful glass selection. The miniature "landscapes" visible in its square "windows" were carefully cut to create the illusion of multiple landscape views. As its name suggests, the design is based on a quilting pattern.

■ TECH TIPS

For the landscape squares, choose glass that will show up well with sunlight behind it.

This panel may be enlarged or reduced by including different numbers of windows (see Figure 1). The photo

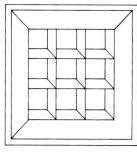

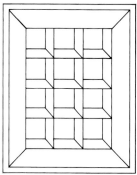

Figure 1

depicts a 15-window panel, in which each 2-3/4"-square (7 cm) landscape is framed by two 1-1/4"-wide (3.2 cm) mitered strips of glass.

To create a full-size assembly pattern, just use the dimensions provided in Figure 2 to draw a grid

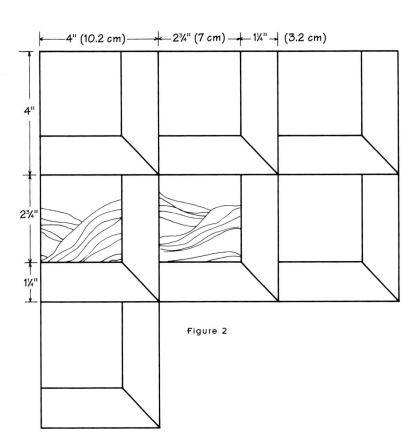

Figure 2

filled with squares. To create cut lines for the four exterior border strips, draw 2"-wide (5.1 cm) borders around the grouped boxes; don't forget to include the mitered corners.

If you choose to lead up this panel rather than foil it, be sure to use the correct pattern shears and refer to "Leading Grids" on page 75.

■ HOOK INSTRUCTIONS

The panel in the photo is suspended from eye hooks screwed into its wooden frame. If you choose not to add the wooden frame, see Steps 15-18 on pages 64-65 for instructions on making hooks for the zinc frame.

SIX-PANEL TABLE LAMP

This six-panel lamp couldn't be any easier to make—or be more economical to cut.

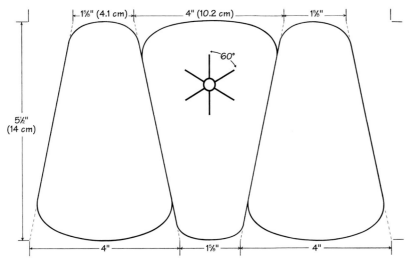

■ AMAZING RHOMBIC BOX

Based on a simple arrangement of geometric forms, this box may be the only project we've included that has the potential to drive you crazy. One hint: Don't try to visualize how the pieces of glass fit together. Instead, cut cardboard templates and tape them together before you begin. The patterns are arranged on the page very much as they're assembled.

■ SPECIAL TOOLS AND MATERIALS

■ See "Making and Attaching Hinges" on page 75.

■ TECH TIPS

Mark your templates to indicate the color streaks in your glass (we've shown their directions in the patterns), and when you remove the templates, mark these grain lines on the glass.

To assemble the box frame, foil and tin all pieces. Then tack together all parts except the lid. Solder the inner and outer seams of the box, and cold solder the border beads on the frame and lid. To attach the lid, refer to the hinge instructions on page 75.

ENLARGE UNTIL EACH SIDE OF EVERY PIECE IS 4" (10.2 CM) LONG.

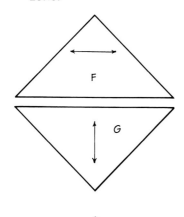

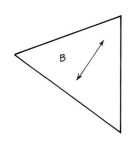

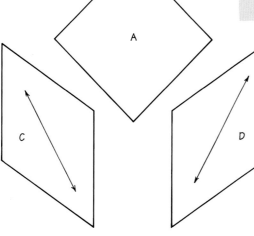

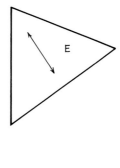

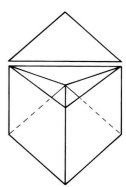

■ CANDLE SURROUNDS

Both these projects include mirrors, which reflect the flames of the candles set inside the three-panel assemblies.

■ SPECIAL TOOLS AND MATERIALS

- Two 6" x 9" (15.2 x 22.9 cm) pieces of mirror, for Surround A
- One 6" x 9" (15.2 x 22.9 cm) piece of mirror, for Surround B
- Clear lacquer or varnish

■ TECH TIPS

See "Protecting Mirrors from Flux and Patina" on page 75.

The two art glass panels in Surround B are mirror images of each other. To cut the glass for these, make two sets of identical templates from the pattern and glue one set to the glass face up, and the other face down. (Be sure to mark the glass pieces after you remove the templates or you may mix up the sets.)

For assembly and soldering tips, read "Lamp Assembly" on pages 75-76.

SURROUND A

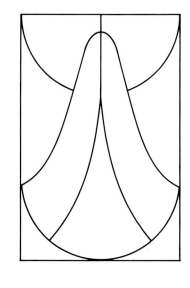

SURROUND B

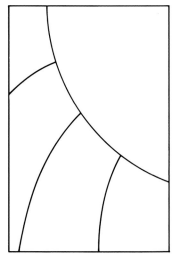

SUGGESTED PANEL SIZE: APPROXIMATELY 6" X 9" (15.2 X 22.9 cm)

◼ FLYING TETRAHEDRON LAMP

You don't need to understand geometry to appreciate this spectacular lamp's graceful lines or ease of assembly. The nine pieces of glass are assembled in sets of three.

◼ SPECIAL TOOLS AND MATERIALS

- See "Making and Attaching Spiders" on page 76.

◼ TECH TIPS

Select a "quiet" glass for the narrower side pieces and a feature glass with a strong pattern or bright colors for the wider ones.

Assemble each of the three panels separately, soldering all seams except those that will be situated between the sets. Then refer to "Lamp Assembly" on pages 75-76.

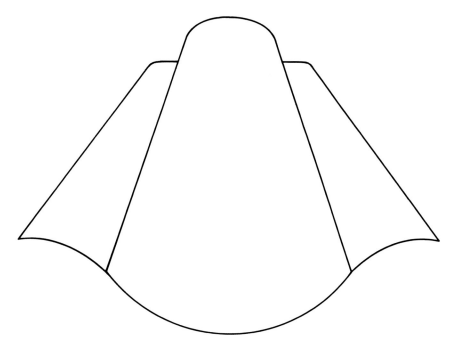

ENLARGE PATTERN 300%.

■ RED EYE LAMP

Remember our hint about using touches of cathedral glass as jewel-like highlights in lamp shades? The red eyes in the panels of this lamp are perfect examples.

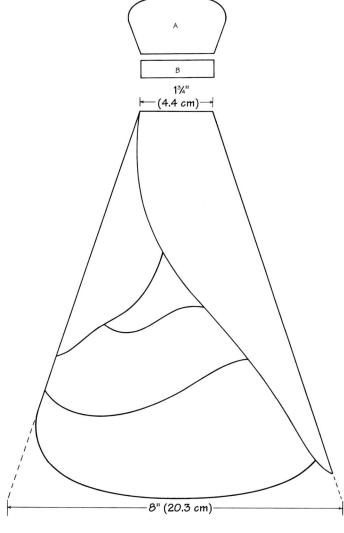

■ SPECIAL TOOLS AND MATERIALS

- See "Making and Attaching Spiders" on page 76.

■ TECH TIPS

Three of the panels in this six-panel lamp are mirror images of the other three. To cut the glass, make six sets of templates and glue three sets to the glass face up, and three face down. Cut six identical crowns (A) and six (optional) collars (B). Assemble each of the six panels separately, soldering all seams except those that will be situated between the sets. Then refer to "Lamp Assembly" on pages 75-76. Attach the optional collars and crowns after the shade has been assembled.

■ PENTAGONAL BOX

The pattern to this charming box may be adjusted to any size; in fact, if you'd like to turn it into a perpendicular-sided plant container, you can. The geometry of the pattern allows for some amazing adjustments.

■ SPECIAL TOOLS AND MATERIALS

- See "Making and Attaching Hinges" on page 75.

■ TECH TIPS

Each side of the pentagonal base of our box is 3" (7.6 cm), but as long as your pentagon is drawn with the correct angles (see the pattern), you can increase or decrease its size as you like. Remember to match the dimensions of the long edges of the box sides to the length of each edge of the base.

Cut five A pieces and one B piece. For a box that isn't tapered (see Figure 1), cut along the solid lines of part A; for a box that is tapered (see photo), cut along the dotted lines of part A. Note that a box without tapers will take a larger lid (see dotted lines in B). To

increase the height of the finished box, just increase the height of Part A to any dimension you choose.

No pattern is provided here for the lid to this box. After you've tacked the A and B pieces together, turn the box upside down onto a piece of glass, and establish cut lines for the lid by marking the box's outline onto the glass blank.

For assembly tips, see "Lamp Assembly" on pages 75-76.

See "Making and Attaching Hinges" on page 75.

If you choose to make a plant container from this box pattern, be sure to line it with waterproof material; a plastic milk container cut to size will work well. Copper foil projects will not hold water!

ENLARGE AS DESIRED

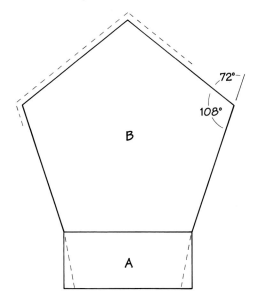

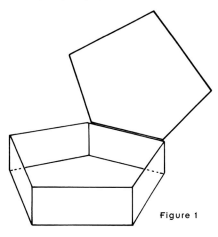

Figure 1

■ CHRYSANTHEMUM CONE LAMP

This elegant lamp can be made in sizes ranging from 8 to 20 panels. You won't need to make any adjustments in the pattern; just cut as many panels as you choose.

■ SPECIAL TOOLS AND MATERIALS

- One vase cap, available from stained-glass suppliers

■ TECH TIPS

Order the vase cap after you've finished assembling the lamp; you'll need to match its size to the size of the shade you've made.

Decide how many panels you'd like to include. To save glass, cut the panels from a long blank, as shown in Figure 1, marking its edges and drawing cutting lines as indicated. Score and break (or grind) the arcs after the panels are cut, using templates if you like.

See "Lamp Assembly" on pages 75-76.

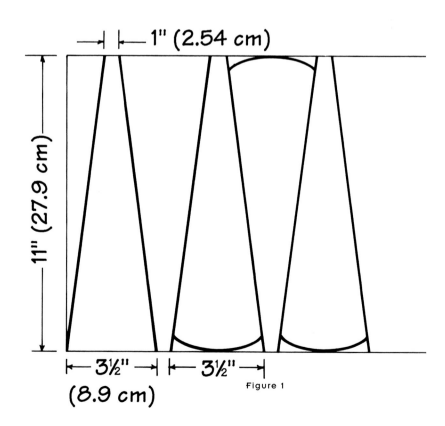

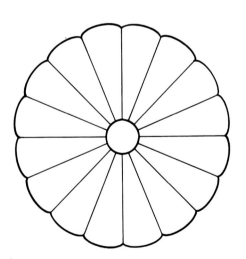

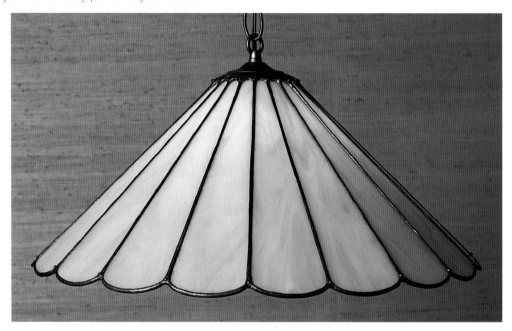

Figure 1

■ KALEIDOSCOPE

This unusual project requires no difficult cuts, but because the construction process is fairly complex, we'll walk you through it step by step.

■ SPECIAL TOOLS AND MATERIALS

- 1'-square (30.5 cm-square) piece of mirror
- 1'-square piece of opaque glass for the body and base
- 6"-square (15.2 cm-square) piece of clear float glass (for pattern A)
- Various pieces of colored textured cathedral glass (for pattern B)
- Sheet of copper foil for overlay at viewing end of body
- 1/8" (3 mm) brass brazing rod
- Brass tubing with an I.D. (inside diameter) large enough to accommodate the brazing rod
- Masking tape
- Glass grinder
- Hot-glue gun and glue sticks
- Brass cleaner
- Black patina

■ WHAT TO DO

1. Cut the following pieces of glass:
Five 1" x 11" (2.5 x 27.9 cm) strips for the body
Three 1-1/4" x 5-1/2" (3.2 x 14 cm) strips for the base
One 2" x 5-1/2" strip for the base
Two of pattern A for the base
Six of pattern B for the wheel
Three 11" x 1-1/6" strips of mirror for the body
2. Cut a 2-3/4" length from the brass brazing rod and a 5/8" (1.6 cm)

length from the brass tubing. Set aside.
3. Foil all the glass pieces except for the mirrors.
4. Place the five 11" body strips face down, lining them up to touch one another. Place two 4-3/4" (12 cm) pieces of masking tape across their backs, at the top and bottom. Now fold the strips into a pentagonal tube. Flux and tack solder the adjoining edges at the top and bottom, squeezing them together as you do to assure a tight fit. (You must avoid allowing any solder to leak into the tube.)
5. Place the pentagonal body on your work surface and tack-solder along the seams, squeezing the strips together as you do. Then tin the seams and fill them each with a smooth bead of solder. Set the body aside.
6. Tack the four base strips together in the same fashion. Then attach the two end pieces (pattern A), and solder all the seams. To help stabilize the kaleidoscope on the base, deposit a small ball of solder on each of the four uppermost corners.
7. Make sure your work surface is clean before starting this step. Position the mirrors with their shiny sides down, leaving gaps as wide as the thickness of a mirror between each pair of strips. Place two 5"-long (12.7 cm) strips of mask-

ing tape across the backs of the mirrors, pressing the tape down firmly to ensure good adhesion and leaving the extra tabs of tape hanging off to one side. Using the free tape ends, pick up the mirrors and turn them over so their shiny sides face up. Clean the shiny surfaces thoroughly, removing all dust. Now pick up the tabs of tape again, and fold the mirrors around to form a closed triangular tube, holding the tube together with the free ends of the tape. Set the tube aside.
8. Clean the scope body (see Step 5) and dry thoroughly. Place one end of the body on the clear glass and trace its outline onto the glass. Repeat to trace the other end. Score and break out the traced glass pieces.
9. Slide the mirror tube into the scope body. You may need to pad the tube to get a snug fit; use scraps of fabric to do this. Secure the mirror to the inside of the body by applying hot glue between the mirrors and the inside walls of the body.
10. Place one of the end pieces over the open end of the body and secure with two small pieces of foil. Then wrap 3/8" (1 cm) copper foil around the end of the body, folding down the foil edges to secure the

end piece in place. Repeat at the other end of the body.
11. To make a triangular viewing hole at one end of the body, place sheet foil over the end piece, masking off the mirrors and leaving only a small triangle of clear glass visible. Before soldering this overlay or the foil at the other end, look through the triangular viewing area; if you see any foil overlapping the mirrors at the opposite end, trim it away with a craft knife.
12. Lightly flux the foil at both ends and apply solder to seal the end pieces in place and to cover the overlay at the viewing end.
13. Arrange the six pieces B to form a circle. The missing point on each piece should create a space in which to house the axle. Solder the pieces together on both surfaces, but be careful not to fill the hole in the center of the circle.
14. To decide which surface of the wheel should face the body of the scope, hold the wheel in front of the scope and view it through the body of the scope. Set the wheel on your work surface with its scope side facing up. Flux the brass tube and place it in the hole in the wheel; the tube must stand upright and square to the wheel. Gently apply solder around the tube to affix it to the wheel.

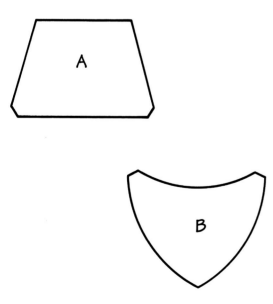

A

B

ENLARGE PATTERN 133%.

15. Flux one end of the rod, and build a small bead of solder at that end. Slip the rod through the tube so that the bead of solder is almost flush with the front of the wheel; the rod should extend back through the wheel and out the tube that rests on the other side of the wheel. Check to see that the wheel spins freely. Then add a small drop of solder to the rod just beyond the point where it extends from the tube. The two beads (one at the end of the rod and one just behind the tube) should keep the wheel from sliding back and forth.

16. Place the wheel assembly on one seam of the scope, aligning the protruding rod with the seam. Hold the rod and spin the wheel to make sure that the wheel doesn't touch the body. Then flux and solder the rod securely to the seam.

17. Clean the outside of the scope with glass cleaner and dry thoroughly. Polish the brass with a brass cleaner. Apply a black patina, rub to a shine, and paint all the solder lines with clear lacquer to preserve their gleaming finish.

■ HEIRLOOM LAMPS

Traditional in design but neverthless striking to the eye, these two hanging lamps are worthy of any room in your home.

ENLARGE PATTERNS 550%.

■ SPECIAL TOOLS AND MATERIALS

■ Vase caps

■ TECH TIPS

See "Lamp Assembly" on pages 75-76.

To ensure a correct fit, purchase your vase caps after you've constructed these lamps.

When assembling the smaller 8-panel lamp, first solder together each set of three small pieces of glass. Next, assemble the large panels to form the basic shape of the lamp; then add the three-piece assemblies one by one.

16-PANEL LAMP

8-PANEL LAMP

■ DON'T SCRAP IT!

After you've made two or three stained glass projects, you'll find yourself with a small box full of scraps too thin to be recut. Save the prettiest ones and use them to make a small free-form panel.

■ SPECIAL TOOLS AND MATERIALS

- ■ 1 nugget

■ TECH TIPS

Draw a rectangle or square on a sheet of craft paper. Position the nugget and trace its outline. Remove the nugget and arrange your scraps within the rectangle, positioning them next to each other in any way you like and cutting as necessary. Once you have an arrangement that pleases you, grind the edges of the scraps to create the spaces necessary to accommodate the copper foil. Trace the outlines of the pieces onto your pattern. (Remember to number both your pattern and scraps.) Then foil the scraps, place them—and the nugget—back on the pattern, and solder the seams. Frame in zinc or brass.

To make the decorative solder beads on the frame, flux the corners of the frame, tin lightly, and deposit three drops of solder onto the tinned area, applying just enough heat to secure each drop of solder.

The artist has framed his piece in 1/2" (1.3 cm) brass channel, mitering each corner for a finished look. Zinc will work just as well.

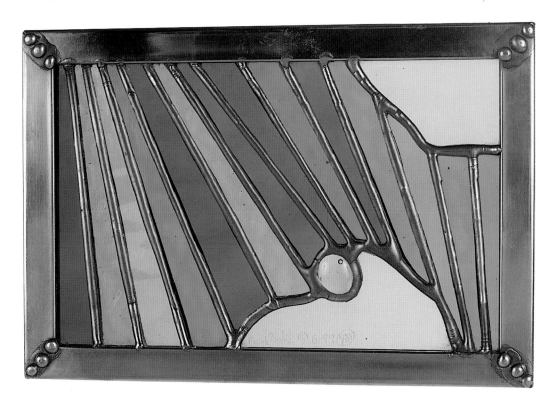

■ HOOK INSTRUCTIONS

See Steps 15-18 on page 64-65, or refer to the hook instructions on page 57.

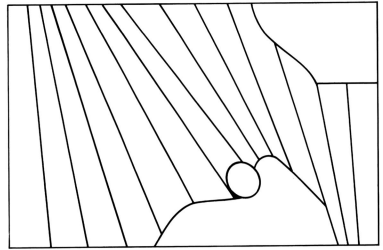

■ BEVEL CLUSTER PANEL

The impressive bevel cluster in this copper foil panel is set off by two textured clear glasses and a touch of color in the border.

■ TECH TIPS

See "Tracing Bevels and Jewels" on page 73. You may lead up this panel if you wish, but don't forget to use the correct shears when you cut your templates!

■ HOOK INSTRUCTIONS

The panel in the photo is framed in wood. If you choose not to add the wooden frame, see Steps 15-18 on pages 64-65 for instructions on making hooks for a zinc frame.

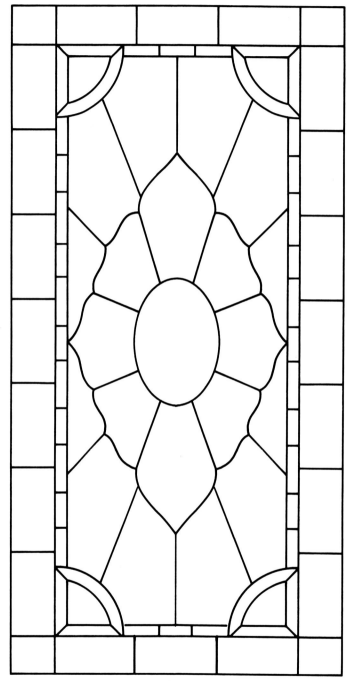

ENLARGE PATTERN 450%.

FISH IN BOWL

Now here's a panel that incorporates copper foil, leading, nuggets, silicone glue, some challenging cuts—and a sense of humor.

ENLARGE PATTERN 400%

SPECIAL TOOLS AND MATERIALS

- Glass grinder with 1/4" (6 mm) bit
- 35 or more nuggets
- 2 nuggets for eyes
- 5 nuggets of different sizes for bubbles
- Lead H-came and U-came for border
- Clear silicone glue
- Medium-gauge copper wire for hooks

TECH TIPS

Before you cut any glass, see "Positioning and Soldering Grouped Nuggets" on page 74.

See "Burnishing Foiled Nuggets" on page 74.

Don't try to score the sharp interior curves. Shape them by using the small bit on your grinder.

The blue border pieces are joined to the interior foiled pieces by H-came, and the outer border of the panel is wrapped in U-came. There's no need to foil the edges of glass that will be hidden by the H-came; foil only the interior edges of these pieces.

Tack together the foiled pieces (those inside the blue border) and solder the seams on that side, but don't run the beads all the way to the border. Next, wrap the soldered pieces with H-came. Then assemble the blue border pieces and the leading between them, and finish by wrapping the exterior of the panel with lead U-came. Solder the joints and solder the beads to the H-came. Turn the panel and solder the other side, but read "Hook Instructions" before you do. Use silicone glue to attach the five clear bubble nuggets to the background glass and the dark nuggets to the eyes.

HOOK INSTRUCTIONS

To make exceptionally strong hooks for this panel, take two lengths of doubled medium-gauge copper wire and bend them to the shapes shown in the pattern. Solder their entire lengths onto the back of the panel, directly on top of the leading and into the seams.

FOLDED CUBIC HANGING LAMP

While it may look complex, this hanging lamp couldn't be any easier to cut or assemble.

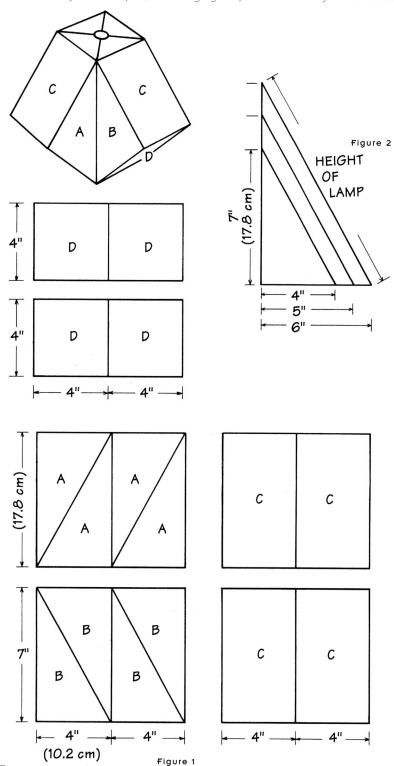

Figure 2

HEIGHT OF LAMP

7" (17.8 cm)

4"
5"
6"

4"

D D

4"

D D

4"   4"

(17.8 cm)

A A
  A   A

B B
B   B

C C

C C

7"

4"   4"
(10.2 cm)

4"   4"

Figure 1

SPECIAL TOOLS AND MATERIALS

- See "Making and Attaching Spiders" on page 76.

TECH TIPS

The lamp consists of four assemblies, each consisting of one piece A, one piece B, one piece C, and one piece D. To save glass, cut the pieces from blanks as shown in Figure 1.

To make a larger lamp shade, just increase the base dimension of 4" (10.2 cm), as shown in Figure 2, and draw parallel lines as indicated to increase the height of the triangular A and B pieces.

Construct each of the four sections separately by tacking and soldering their interior and exterior seams, cold-soldering the top and bottom borders, and tinning the foil that will form the seams between assemblies. Then solder the four assemblies together; you'll find useful tips in "Lamp Assembly" on pages 75-76.

■ BEVEL ARRANGEMENT

The design possibilities inherent in bevels are almost limitless. Try out a few. Arrange an assortment of bevels on a large sheet of paper until their placement pleases you. Trace the outline of each bevel onto the paper, and sketch in cut lines to divide the spaces around them.

■ TECH TIPS

■ See "Tracing Bevels and Jewels" on page 73.

■ HOOK INSTRUCTIONS

The panel shown in the photo is suspended from hooks screwed into a wooden frame. A good cabinetmaker can construct a wooden frame for your zinc-framed panel, but if you'd like to avoid this extra expense, frame your panel in zinc alone and refer to Steps 15-18 on pages 64-65 for instructions on making hooks.

ENLARGE PANEL 650%

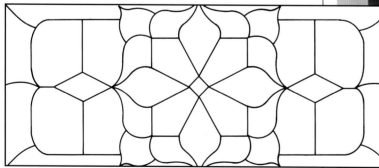

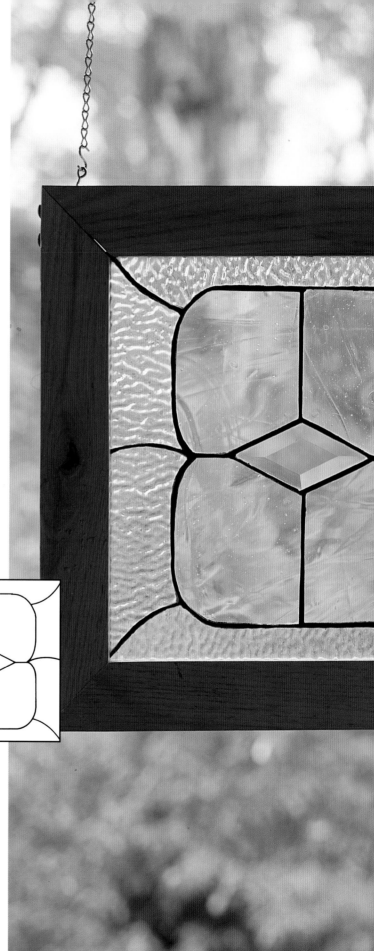

■ HOUSE FOR JEWELS

The artist who designed this leaded panel demonstrates conclusively that a pattern doesn't have to be complex to yield a fascinating finished piece. By combining bevels, jewels, and textured clear glass with an unusual glass-free space, she's created a surprisingly sophisticated design.

■ SPECIAL TOOLS AND MATERIALS

- Four 1-1/2"-square (3.8 cm) bevels
- Three 1" x 10" (2.5 x 25.4 cm) bevels
- One 5-7/8" x 1-3/8" (14.9 x 3.5 cm) bevel
- One 6-3/8" x 1" (16.2 x 2.5 cm) bevel
- One 7-7/8" x 1" (20 x 2.5 cm) bevel
- Two 1"-diameter (2.5 cm) jewels
- One 5/8"-diameter (1.6 cm) jewel
- One 1/2"-diameter (1.3 cm) jewel

■ TECH TIPS

See "Tracing Bevels and Jewels" on page 73.

See "Leading Round Jewels" on page 73..

The purple jewel (see upper left of panel in photo) was placed just slightly off-center. To change the pattern we've provided, place your jewel about 1/4" (6 mm) to the left of its pattern location and trace around it.

Unless you plan to have this panel installed, we recommend framing it in 1/4" (6 mm) zinc U-came rather than lead.

■ HOOK INSTRUCTIONS

See Steps 15-18 on pages 64-65.

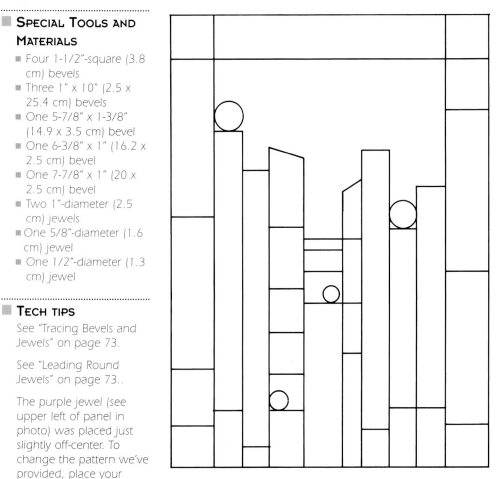

ENLARGE PANEL 325%

STUDY IN LINES AND CIRCLES

This carefully designed panel is a fine example of the ways in which combinations of relatively simple cut lines and wise glass selection can create a stunning work. You may very well want to adjust the dimensions and design to fit a window in your home.

◼ SPECIAL TOOLS AND MATERIALS

- ▪ One 3" x 3" (7.6 x 7.6 cm) square bevel
- ▪ One 5"-diameter (12.7 cm) half-circle bevel
- ▪ One 3"-diameter semicircular bevel
- ▪ One 3"-radius quarter circle bevel
- ▪ Five diamond bevels (optional) with 1-3/4" (4.4 cm) edges
- ▪ One 4-1/4"-diameter (10.8 cm) rondel

◼ TECH TIPS

Feel free to substitute art glass for any of the bevels used in this piece. See "Tracing Bevels and Jewels" on page 73. Remember, the design can be adjusted to fit the bevels and rondel you purchase.

◼ HOOK INSTRUCTIONS

This panel has been framed in wood and is suspended by means of eyehooks inserted into the frame. Any good cabinetmaker should be able to create a wooden frame for you, but you may also use zinc U-came and create hooks as described in Steps 15-18 on pages 64-65.

ENLARGE PATTERN 700%

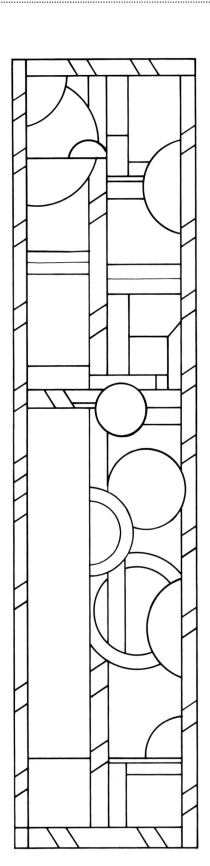

Chapter Eleven: Gallery

Stained-glass artists—the men and women whose work can be found in churches, homes, businesses, galleries, and museums around the world—are very special people. As different as they are from one another, they all share the remarkable ability to use glass as a personal language, one that gives voice both to the beauty around them and to their innermost visions.

In this section, you'll find photos of some remarkable works by remarkable people. Luxuriate in these pieces, by all means. Let them speak to you. Refer to them when your own muse seems to be on vacation and you need an inspiring lift, but do remember, please, not to copy these designs. We trust you'll be able to enjoy them without succumbing to excessive envy—or breaking copyright laws!

Room divider

Nancy Sledd and Mary Lu Winger

Above: Fireplace cover
Left: Room divider
Below: Fireplace screen
Nancy Sledd and Mary Lu Winger

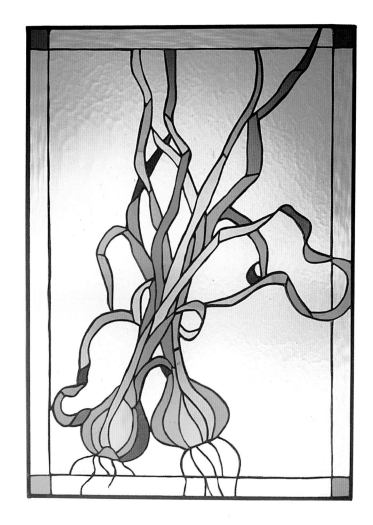

Above: Oval panel with geodes
Martha Mitchell and Rachel Ward

Upper right: Onion panel
Roberta Katz-Messenger

Right: Corner panels
Lorn Marshall

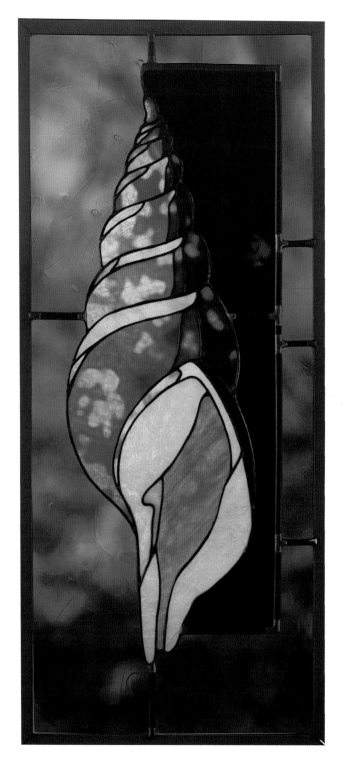

Left: Seashell panel
Upper right: Sun and moon panel
Above: Sun panel
Martha Mitchell and Rachel Ward

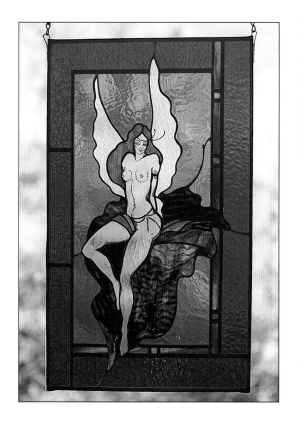

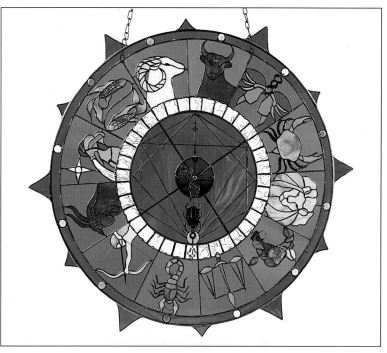

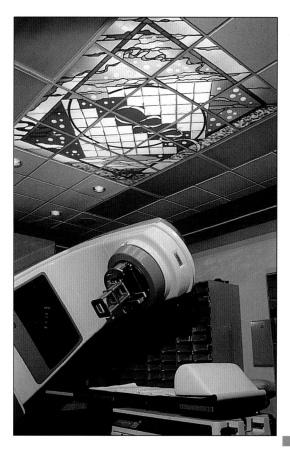

Upper left: Fairy panel
Martha Mitchell and Rachel Ward

Upper right: Night Sky panel
Debra and Bob Strack
Photographer: Miles Burns

Above: Glass wall
Virginia Hoffman

Right: Ceiling panels in radiation treatment room
Virginia Hoffman

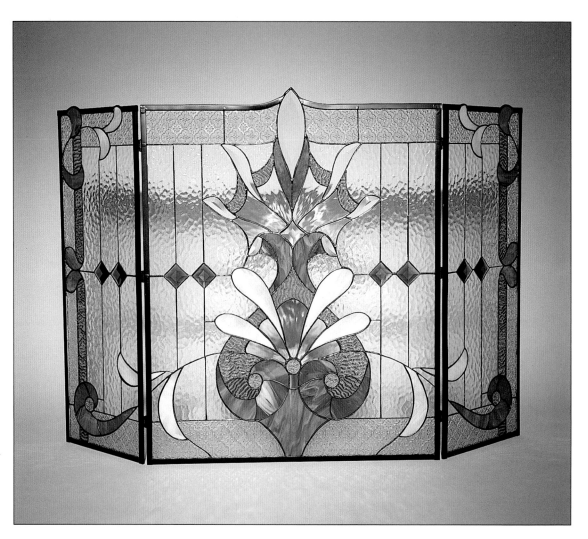

Fireplace
screens

Nancy Sledd
and Mary Lu
Winger

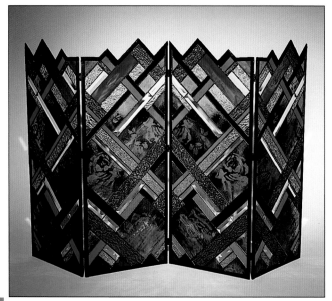

Upper left: Heron panel
Roberta Katz-Messenger

Upper right: Room divider
Roberta Katz-Messenger

Above and right: Lamps
Gene Messick

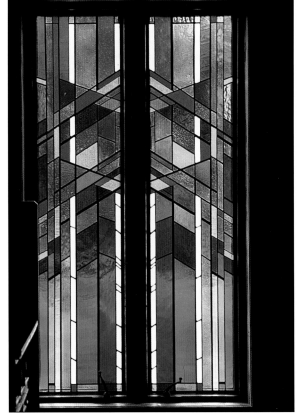

Above: Window
Upper right: Entrance doors
Lower right: Windows
Lou Ellen Beckham-Davis

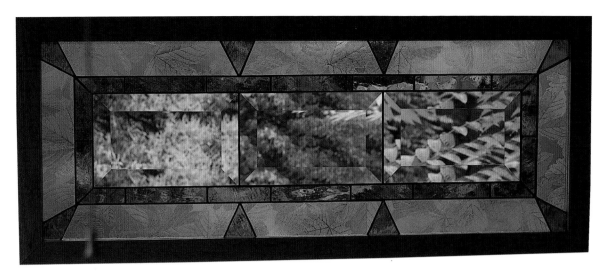

Top: Three-bevel panel

Left: Floral panel

Above: Bevel panel

Bob Pace

Upper right: Leaded glass side lites, door inserts,
and transoms
Virginia Hoffman

Lower left: Strawberry panel
Roberta Katz-Messenger

Above: Leaded glass inserts for front doors
Virginia Hoffman

Upper left: Sea-serpent lamp
Debra and Bob Strack
Photographer: Miles Burns

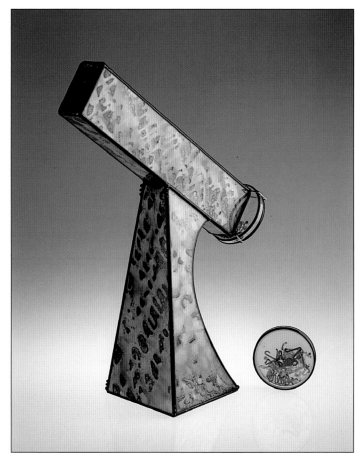

Upper left: Senet (Egyptian board game)
Debra and Bob Strack

Upper right: Kaleidoscope
Debra and Bob Strack

Left: Parlour Implosion (kaleidoscope)
Marc Tickle

Above: The Pinnacle (kaleidoscope)
Marc Tickle

METRIC CONVERSION CHARTS

Inches	CM	Inches	CM
1/8	0.3	20	50.8
1/4	0.6	21	53.3
3/8	1.0	22	55.9
1/2	1.3	23	58.4
5/8	1.6	24	61.0
3/4	1.9	25	63.5
7/8	2.2	26	66.0
1	2.5	27	68.6
1-1/4	3.2	28	71.1
1-1/2	3.8	29	73.7
1-3/4	4.4	30	76.2
2	5.1	31	78.7
2-1/2	6.4	32	81.3
3	7.6	33	83.8
3-1/2	8.9	34	86.4
4	10.2	35	88.9
4-1/2	11.4	36	91.4
5	12.7	37	94.0
6	15.2	38	96.5
7	17.8	39	99.1
8	20.3	40	101.6
9	22.9	41	104.1
10	25.4	42	106.7
11	27.9	43	109.2
12	30.5	44	111.8
13	33.0	45	114.3
14	35.6	46	116.8
15	38.1	47	119.4
16	40.6	48	121.9
17	43.2	49	124.5
18	45.7	50	127.0
19	48.3		

Volumes		Weights	
1 fluid ounce	29.6 ml	0.035 ounces	1 gram
1 pint	473 ml	1 ounce	28.35 grams
1 quart	946 ml	1 pound	453.6 grams
1 gallon (128 fl. oz.)	3.785 l		

ACKNOWLEDGEMENTS

The authors are indebted to the stained glass artists who contributed to this book. Without their patience, generosity, and skills, Stained Glass Basics would not exist.

Steve Brewer

(pages 45, 78-79, and 122-23), glass artisan and repairman extraordinaire, was kind enough to write Chapter Nine. A past student of Marty's, Steve does some work for A Touch of Glass in Asheville, North Carolina, and also does "lamp work" (melting glass with a torch to form and shape it) at his home studio, where he creates a variety of glass creatures.

Lou Ellen Beckham-Davis

(pages 13, 82, 128-129, and 138) designs commissioned pieces for architectural installation. She lives with her husband and son in Greenville, South Carolina, where she does business under the name of L.E.B. Glass Studio. Thank you, Lou Ellen, for making our photography sessions so much easier than they might have been.

Virginia Hoffman

(pages 135 and 140), who works in Sarasota, Florida, designs and creates site-specific architectural and ornamental pieces for a wide range of clientele, including banks, corporations, schools, churches, hotels, residences, and restaurants. Photographs of her award-winning works (the designs for which are copyrighted, so do refrain from copying the ones in this book) have appeared in national and international magazines. We're proud to be able to include a few in **Stained Glass Basics**.

Roberta Katz-Messenger

(pages 58, 86, 87, 133, 137, and 140), who has been a stained glass artist since 1970, owns Pentacle Studio— a gallery of fine arts, crafts, and gifts in Clinton, Arkansas. Roberta makes a special effort to collect the finest of work by residents of her state; the gallery has been called one of the two best in Arkansas. Her prize-winning stained glass designs are in both public and private collections. We're especially grateful to Roberta for her remarkable ability to maintain a sense of humor under duress.

Lorn Marshall

(pages 119 and 133), who describes himself as an "old artist, craftsman, inventor, guru, and gizmo maker," has been working with glass, metal, and wood for 22 years. Lorn operates Fanglasstic and Friends in Greenville, South Carolina.

Steve McLester

the skilled glass artist and true gentleman who made the panel shown on the cover of this book, has been a glass artist since 1985. Steve owns Asheville Stained Glass and Sandblasting in Asheville, North Carolina, where he designs and fabricates windows for installation in a wide range of styles, including Arts and Crafts. Thank you, Steve, for stepping in with the perfect panel at the perfect time.

Gene Messick

(pages 24, 104-115, 124-125, and 137) owns Lightworks Studio (P.O. Box 495, Earl, North Carolina) where he teaches stained glass crafts, creates fused and copper foil pieces, and sells lamp supplies. We can't thank Gene enough for his multiple trips to Asheville, for his ability to survive Chris's attacks of writer's anxiety, or for his technical advice. Gene's works are all copyrighted; do write to ask his permission before copying any of his projects for sale or before copying any of his gallery designs.

Gary Newlin

is the owner of A Touch of Glass in Asheville, North Carolina and the author of **Simple Kaleidoscopes** (Sterling/Lark, 1995). By generously opening his studio space to a number of local artists, Gary has allowed them to discover their own ways of pursuing their love affair with glass. As a group, we'd like to thank him for the use of his studio and for his sound advice.

Bob Pace

(pages 5, 71, 96-97, 98-99, 118, 120-121, 126-127, 130, and 139) is a native of western North Carolina and a self-taught artist who has been working in stained glass for 25 years. For the past 17 of those years, he has owned and operated The Riverwood Menagerie, his studio in Dillsboro, North Carolina. Bob specializes in custom orders for churches, private homes, and businesses in the Southeast.

Nancy Sledd and Mary Lu Winger

(pages 131, 132, and 136), who are listed in the 1993 **Who's Who in American Crafts**, have been working with glass for two decades. Their distinctive stained glass firescreens, panels, and room dividers have won numerous awards, are shown in museums and galleries throughout the United States, and are offered in national and international catalogues. Collectors of their work include novelist Stephen King and NBA star John Newman. Their work was also selected for the 1993 White House Christmas Tree in celebration of the Year of American Craft. Their business, Sledd/Winger Glassworks, is located in Richmand, Virginia.

Dana Stegall

(pages 102-103) is a self-taught glass artist who owns The Glass Shoppe in Clayton, Georgia, where she creates windows, lamps, music boxes, suncatchers, and custom orders.

Debra and Bob Strack

(pages 71, 80, 83-85, 100-101, 135, 140, and 141) live with their dogs and cats in an old farm house on the outskirts of Conway, Arkansas. The two have been working in stained glass since 1983, but have never desired to form a business. They prefer to have the freedom to pursue their own interest in design. Most of their work is naturalistic and is often based on the flowers and wildlife on their property. Their glass work, which is occasionally influenced by their other passions—turn-of-the-century art glass and antiques—also includes art nouveau windows and replicas of Tiffany lamps.

The photographs of their pieces on pages 135 and 140 were taken by photographer Miles Burns.

Marc Tickle

(pages 116-117 and 141) handcrafts some of the finest glass kaleidoscopes we've ever seen. His business, On Reflection, is based in the south of England, but Marc spends a significant amount of time in Asheville, North Carolina. He returns to England periodically to monitor his business operations there.

Thanks also to:

Dana Irwin, the art director at Altamont Press who transformed our text and images into a work of art.

Evan Bracken (Light Reflections, Hendersonville, North Carolina), whose photographs make these pages come alive.

Orrin Lundgren, our illustrator, who not only produced an amazing amount of work in a very short period of time, but who also acquired a love of glass as he did so.

Georgia, who first taught Marty the craft of stained glass.

Rachel's family, who collectively encouraged and nurtured her love of art and glass.

Chris's parents, who passed along the writer's genes and the sense of humor necessary to survive them.

The pieces shown on pages 7, 71, 74, 75, 77, 81, 88-89, 92-93, 94-95, 133, 134, 135 were designed and made by Martha Mitchell and Rachel Ward.

INDEX

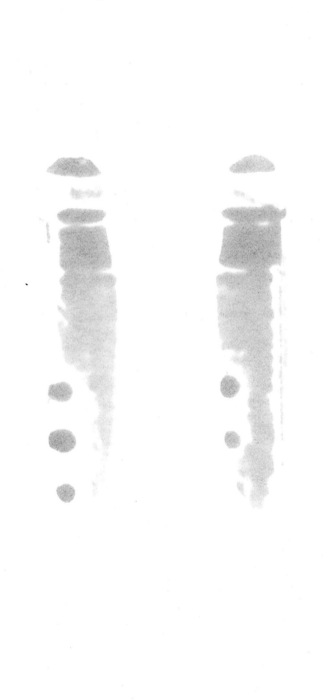